B. Danaher

English Alive!

An Introduction to Communication and Everyday English

Angela Collins and Eilís Leddy

GILL & MACMILLAN

Published in Ireland by
Gill & Macmillan Ltd
Goldenbridge
Dublin 8
with associated companies throughout the world
© Angela Collins and Eilís Leddy 1993
Artwork and Design by Ed Miliano
0 7171 2042 2
Print origination in Ireland by
Seton Music Graphics Ltd, Bantry, Co. Cork
Printed in Ireland by ColourBooks Ltd, Dublin

Contents

Acknowledgments

1.	Television	1
2.	Holidays	20
3.	Mind Your Own Business	42
4.	Fundraising	56
5.	Stereotyping	63
6.	World of Work	81
7.	Newspapers	101
8.	Motoring	116
9.	You, Your Rights and The Law	139
10.	Consumer Affairs and Assertiveness	155
11.	Language	168

Acknowledgments

The authors and publishers thank the following for permission to use copyright material and/or for supplying material for reproduction in the book:

p.13 Topham Picture Source; p.14 Radio Telefis Eireann Illustrations Library; pp.18,19 Allen & Unwin, Sydney; p.23 Ulster Bank Limited; pp.26,27,28 Irish Youth Hostel Association/An Oige; p.28 Youth Hostel Association of Northern Ireland; pp.29,30,31 USIT; pp.34,35,36,37 Passport Office; p.55 *The Manager* magazine for 'The Hot Dog Story'; p.67 Penguin Books Ltd for the extract 'The Little Girl and the Wolf' from *Fables From Our Time* by James Thurber; pp.68,69,70 Attic Press, Dublin for 'Ms Snow White Wins Case in High Court' by Clodagh Corcoran from *Sweeping Beauties*; p.72 *Big!*, *Match*, *M&J*, *Eagle*, *Bunty* and *The Dandy* magazines; pp.73,80 D.C. Thomson & Co., Dundee for 'Roger the Dodger' from *Beano* magazine; p.76 Mary Cummins/The Irish Times; pp.108,109 Cork Examiner; p.108 The Irish Times, Irish Independent; pp.120,121,123,127,128 Department of the Environment for provisional driving licence and extracts from *Rules of the Road*; p.134 Automobile Association; p.150 Irish Society for the Prevention of Cruelty to Children; pp.152,153,154 Allison & Busby for 'Saw it in the papers' by Adrian Mitchell; p.161 *Consumer Choice* magazine for 'Ten tips on how to complain'.

Every effort has been made to trace copyright holders but if any have been overlooked inadvertently the publishers will be pleased to make the necessary arrangements at the first opportunity.

Unit One—Television

Introducing Television

You are probably surprised to see a unit on television in your text-book. No doubt you think that all you need to know about television is how to switch it on and then at the end of the evening's viewing how to switch it off. However, there's far more to it than that! The aim of television is to *entertain*, to *educate* and to *inform*. All the time that you are watching television you are receiving messages whether you are aware of the fact or not. Many of the most subtle messages are received subconsciously. It is important that you should be able to interpret and understand the messages.

Background

The word 'television' comes from the Greek *tele* meaning 'far' and *visio* which is the Latin word for 'sight'. So the word 'television' means 'seeing at a distance'. The purpose of a television system is to extend the senses of vision and hearing beyond their natural limits. Do you think that 'television' is an appropriate name for the box on which we watch moving images? Although it is quite difficult to think of another word, can you suggest an alternative name to 'television'?

Although many scientists have attempted to develop a television system it was the Scottish scientist John Logie Baird who, in 1926, gave the first demonstration of true television by electrically transmitting moving pictures. The results were crude but became the start of television as we know it. On 2 November 1936, the world's first public television broadcast was transmitted by the British Broadcasting Corporation (BBC) from Alexandra Palace in London. The broadcast was received by just 100 sets. We have come a long way since then. Today, there are over 250 million television sets in the world.

A lot of the old myths about television have been exploded now that we all take television for granted. You may have heard the expression 'square eyes'. Some people actually used to believe that if you spent too long staring at television it would affect your eyes: they thought that you might actually become square-eyed from looking at the square screen.

It is true to say that television has revolutionised our lives. It has also made us lazier. Before television, people had to make their own entertainment—they read books, played cards, listened to the radio and, most importantly, they talked to one another, they engaged in conversation.

Most households today have at least one television set. Do a quick survey of your group. How many people *don't* have a television at home? It is unlikely that there will be more than a few. Although you will probably find that most people do own a television set there is still a sizeable minority of people who *choose* not to have a set. To most of you the advantages of owning a set will be immediately obvious but try to think about the disadvantages of owning a set.

- Draw up a list of at least three advantages to owning a set and three disadvantages.

- Discuss these advantages and disadvantages with your group.

Remember it is easy to say that you can be selective about the programmes you watch but in practice in most homes once the television has been switched on it is rarely switched off until the evening's viewing is at an end. How often have you sat with the television on just flicking from channel to channel because there's absolutely nothing on that interests you? There are some people who would say that the invention of remote control was a cruel joke, a subtle torture device!

It is enormously expensive to make television programmes so who pays for them? There are a number of different ways in which the money can be raised.

1. Licence fee Every person who has a television set at home is obliged by law to buy a television licence. Failure to have such a licence can result in a large fine.

2. Rental of piped television   The rental is usually collected every quarter by whichever company has the local franchise. Franchise means the right to sell the goods or services of a company in a particular area.

3. Satellite   Although you may feel that the price you pay for the use of your television is far too high, particularly when you have little interest in many of the programmes which are shown, still you must remember that this money is only a tiny proportion of the money required to make television programmes.

4. Advertising   Television companies get most of their revenue (money) from advertising.

When you consider how many millions of people see television advertisements, it is not surprising that advertising companies are prepared to spend vast amounts of money to advertise their products on prime time television. Because television advertisements are both visual and aural they create a greater impact than advertisements which are merely visual or aural.

Those of you who receive BBC television know that there is no advertising on either of the channels. BBC is state funded so the tax payer pays for it indirectly.

Programme Selection

'You cannot satisfy all of the people all of the time.' Although you may think that there is nothing worth watching on television someone else might well be delighted with the range of programmes, as in the old saying, 'One man's meat is another man's poison.'

It is the job of the **Controller of Programmes** to see that there is a wide variety of programmes which will cater to many different tastes. Channel 4 in particular tends to show programmes which have a definite minority appeal.

Do you think this is fair?

Do you agree that minority interests such as bowls, scrabble, tap dancing and butterfly collecting should have their own programmes on television despite being of little interest to the majority of viewers?

You will appreciate that it is quite difficult to strike a balance. Although it might be your idea of a perfect night's viewing to watch three consecutive hours of a tiddlywinks tournament, it is unlikely to appeal to everyone else.

Tonight's Viewing

6.05	Home and Away
6.35	Neighbours
7.00	Home and Away
7.30	The Bill
8.00	Glenroe
8.30	Caber Tossing Finals
9.00	Live Open Heart Surgery
9.30	Home and Away
10.00	Neighbours
10.30	News
10.32	Fair City
11.00	Yoga Relaxation (for those of you who aren't already unconscious)
11.30	Cattle Mart Report

This may be someone's idea of a great night's viewing but do you think that there are many people who could bear to spend their night watching the above?

- Imagine that you are the Controller of Programmes. Look at the television guide for the week. You may use any programmes from any channel. Try to compile one night's viewing which you feel will satisfy most people.

- Look at the television guide overleaf. It lists all the programmes available to you on all the channels.

RTE 1

6.00 The Angelus

6.01 Six-One

and

Weatherline

followed by

News for the Deaf

6.57 Time Out

A time to stop and reflect for two minutes on some of the important questions of our lives.

7.00 Know Your Sport

Sports quiz presented by George Hamilton with Memory Man Jimmy Magee.

7.30 Lovejoy

Part one of a two-part episode

Highland Fling

A visit to the Highlands lands Lovejoy in a mystery of missing furniture and ancient frescoes.

8.30 Taking Stock

Victims of Progress

Farmers whose scale of operation is too small to cope with free-market conditions.

9.00 The Nine O'Clock News and Weatherline

9.30 Homefront

Lemo Tomato Juice Hour. Linda's newspaper editorial opens up a whole new world.

10.25 Questions and Answers

John Bowman chairs the current affairs debate.

11.30 Late News

followed by

A Prayer at Bedtime

Transmission ends at 11.40pm*

NETWORK 2

6.05 JMTV Magazine

Evening Ireland! Start your week here in Studio 5 with JMTV's Celine, Colin Shauna.

6.30 Home and Away

Bobby waits as her father hovers between life and death.

7.00 Nuacht

7.08 Cúrsaí

Tus bríomhair don tseachtain. Beoscealta thall is abhus á gcur i láthair ag Bridóg Ní Bhuachalla agus Pat Butler.

7.30 Coronation Street

Doug receives a huge boost to his morale but needs a friend to make his dreams come true.

8.00 News Headlines and Weatherline

8.05 Blackboard Jungle

Presenter: Ray D'Arcy
Design: Pat Molloy
Directed by Ian McGarry
Producer: Gerald Heffernan

8.30 Eerie Indiana

No Fun

Simon turns into a workaholic

9.00 Cheers

Carla has to take a job at another pub.

9.30 News Headlines

followed by

Italian Football

10.30 Network News and Weatherline

10.50 Larry Gogan's Video Golden Oldies

The Peter Pan of Pop returns to your screens with 30 years of pop and rock.

Transmission ends at 11.50pm*

BBC 1

6:00 Six O'Clock News; Weather

6:30 Neighbours

6:57 Inside Ulster News

7:00 Eldorado

7:30 Watchdog

8:00 Grace and Favour

8:30 Punch-Drunk

"Vendetta" Kenny Ireland, Diana Hardcastle, John Kazek. Norman Banks MD is dedicated to helping his fellow man – as long as he's not called Vinnie Binns. (Ceefax) (Nicam Digital Stereo)

9:00 Nine O'Clock News; Regional News; Weather

(Ceefax)

9:30 Panorama

Vigorous investigation of a topical issue.

10:10 Art on Film

"Between Heaven and Woolworths". A host of Irish literary celebrities, including John Banville, Tom Murphy and Neil Jordan, offer their insights into the art of story-telling.

11:05 Film 93 with Barry Norman

The latest film version of 'Dracula' stars Gary Oldman, Anthony Hopkins and Winona Ryder and is based closely on Bram Stoker's novel.

11:35 Match of the Day – The Road to Wembley

Tony Gubba and Trevor Brooking with action from to-night's FA Cup fourth round tie.

12:25 Careering Ahead

BBC 2

6:00 The Addams Family

"The Winning of Morticia Addams". Follow the comic adventures of the ghoulish Addams family.

6:25 Def II: The Fresh Prince of Bel Air

"Here Comes the Judge" Starring Will Smith.

6:50 Def II: Cyberzone

7:20 The Name of the Room

8:00 Horizon

8:50 Sean's Shorts

Comedian Sean Hughes travels the UK, arriving in the ancient university city of Oxford.

9:00 Film: "Doing Life"

10:30 Newsnight

11:15 The Late Show

"Russian Week"

UTV

6:00 UTV Live at Six

7:00 Wish You Were Here . . .?

7:30 Coronation Street

Doug receives a huge boost to his morale. (Oracle)

7:59 UTV Live News Update

8.00 The Upper Hand

8:30 World in Action

Three miners from different areas of Britain are given the chance to launch their own investigation into the pit crisis.

8.59 UTV Live News Update

9:00 Head Over Heels

10:00 News at Ten; Weather (Oracle)

10:30 UTV Live: The 10.30 News

Local news.
(Followed by Local Weather)

10.40 Viewpoint 93

"A Murder in Mind". An insight into the lives of serial killers and the investigators who hunt them. Featuring interviews with the murderers themselves and unprecedented police access in Britain, America and Russia, it reveals the mysteries of psychological profiling and the real-life 'Silence of the Lambs' cases.

11:10 Film: "The Devil's Daughter"

CHANNEL 4

6:00 Roseanne

6:30 The Cosby Show

7:00 Channel 4 News; Weather

7:50 Comment

8:00 Brookside

8:30 Desmond's

9:00 Cutting Edge

10:00 Northern Exposure

11:00 Writing on the Line

12:00 Hollywood Legends

"Gary Cooper – American Life, American Legend"

Think very carefully before compiling your evening's viewing.

When the Controller of Programmes is planning the order in which programmes will be shown s/he has to think about **targeting** and **scheduling**, i.e. choosing the order of programmes to fit in with certain time slots and attract certain audiences.

- It would be foolish to show an hour of cartoons at 10.00 p.m. but can you see any pattern in the way that programmes have been selected?

- Look at the programmes offered in the morning. Who do you think these morning programmes are aimed at?

- Why do you think a 'blockbuster' film is never shown on morning television?

- Look at the television guide again. Examine the way the strongest programme on one channel is pitted against a strong programme on another channel. Why do you think this happens?

- Many newspapers' TV page will recommend programmes in the form of critics' choice. Do you think this is acceptable?

- Write a short paragraph on either the advantages or disadvantages of allowing a critics' choice. Are there any ways in which this could be abused?

It has been said that 'Television is the great unpaid baby-sitter.'

What do you think is meant by this? Would you agree?

The function of television is to entertain but it also manipulates. Are there any dangers involved in allowing a child watch too much children's television? We are all familiar with cartoons such as *Tom and Jerry, Sylvester and Tweety Pie, Bugs Bunny and Elmer Fudd, Tazmania* and *The Simpsons*.

Many people would say that these programmes are amusing and light-hearted and make children laugh. However, it cannot be denied that there is a lot of violence in some of them. Whilst the characters seldom suffer any 'real' hurt it can be argued that young children learn from what they see.

Do you feel that over-exposure to violence could, in some way, be damaging to children? It is accepted that all children love to hear stories and that many children inhabit, at times, a fantasy world. In the past, most parents either told their children stories or read aloud to them. Quite often these story sessions took place at bedtime with the child sitting on the adult's lap. Many of the old fairy stories can be quite frightening and, whilst children enjoy a degree of fear, they are reassured by the physical closeness of a trusted adult. Contrast the image of the child secure on its grandad's lap with a three-year-old child sitting alone watching *Ninja Turtles*.

You might find it interesting to compare a nursery tale with a modern cartoon. Although the characters will be presented differently, you will probably find that there is a goodie and a baddie and that there is usually a fight between good and evil, in which good always triumphs.

 Draw up a chart looking at three fairy tales and three modern cartoons and see whether they are, in fact, similar. Use the following headings.

Cartoons   *Fairy Tales*   *Characters*   *Themes*

Another obvious disadvantage of too much television is that it has made young people lazier both mentally and physically. They no longer have to make their own entertainment and their search for adventure is now satisfied by watching the exploits of television characters such as *The A-Team*, and *MacGyver*.

They have become almost like sponges passively absorbing the ideas portrayed on the screen. Too much of young people's viewing tends to be uncritical. In America, the term *couch potato* has been used to describe a person who uncritically watches too much television. Do you think that this is a good description? Why?

Can you think of any other appropriate names?

You may agree with many of the views expressed or you may, by now, be furious and wish to challenge them.

Prepare a three-minute speech in support of or against the view that 'Television is the Great Unpaid Baby-Sitter'. You should *record* your speech. You might discover when you play it back that your arguments were not as logical or as clearly expressed as you would have hoped.

Remember that when you give a speech you are addressing an audience who may not share your views. The aim of your speech is to persuade them that yours is the correct opinion, so be decisive. Do not, however, confuse decisiveness with bullying and hectoring. Listen to the speeches of your classmates and, where necessary, offer constructive criticism or comment.

Many adults are concerned about the dangers of showing programmes which contain explicit scenes of sex and violence. However, we must be careful not to lump the two together. A scene on television of a couple engaged in sexual intercourse will definitely offend some people but there is no evidence to suggest that it can harm them. However, studies have proven that watching scenes of gratuitous* violence has long-term damaging psychological effects. One has only to read accounts of atrocities committed by lone deranged gunmen who claim that their behaviour has been influenced by what they have seen on television or on film.

Where scenes of sexual violence are shown, studies have again proved that long-term psychological damage can be caused. Scenes showing rape or other brutal assaults can have no justification. Women, in particular, are made to feel vulnerable and many disturbed men may feel that this type of behaviour is in some way acceptable.

Despite the fact that people are aware of the harm that watching such programmes can cause, many feel that their viewers should have the right to choose what they watch. To protect children from such programmes, television companies have agreed on a 9.00 p.m. **watershed** policy. This means that no programmes containing unsuitable material should be broadcast before 9.00 p.m.

Realistically, very few teenagers go to bed at 9.00 p.m. so their choice of viewing should be guided by their parents or guardians.

It is always important to be selective in your viewing.

Look at tonight's television guide. Select the programmes which you would like to watch. Do any of the programme times clash?

Make out a chart of those programmes you would like to watch and the times at which they are shown. You may be surprised how few programmes really interest you.

* 'Gratuitous' means uncalled for, unwarranted, motiveless.

Being selective means making an *informed choice* in advance rather than thoughtlessly staring at a programme which doesn't interest you or zapping aimlessly from one channel to another.

It is obviously vitally important for programme makers to know whether or not their programmes are successful. They can find out this information through an Audience Research Board. Each week figures are released showing how many viewers have watched each programme. These figures are known as TAM* ratings. If a programme is not attracting a wide audience it may be dropped entirely from the schedule.

Look at the TAM ratings for the week ending 3 January 1993:

TAM
The Top Twenty ratings for the week ending 3 January 1993

RTE 1	Day	Viewers in Thousands	Network 2	Day	Viewers in Thousands
1 Glenroe	Sun	1290	1 Home and Away	Wed	730
2 Winning Streak	Fri	947	2 Home and Away	Thurs	697
3 Where in the World	Sun	830	3 Home and Away	Tues	684
4 Shirley Valentine	Thurs	682	4 Coronation Street	Wed	682
5 Golden Fiddles	Sun	663	5 Home and Away	Mon	618
6 National Entert. Awards	Tues	661	6 Home and Away	Fri	581
7 Hunt For Red October	Mon	640	7 Coronation Street	Mon	548
8 Fair City	Thurs	639	8 Blackboard Jungle	Wed	512
9 The Sporting Year	Fri	632	9 Beverly Hills 90210	Tues	490
10 School Around the Corner	Sun	632	10 Coronation Street	Fri	445
11 Fair City	Tues	628	11 Blackboard Jungle	Fri	383
12 Know Your Sport	Mon	544	12 Greenpeace	Wed	364
13 Wonder Years	Sun	538	13 Blackboard Jungle	Mon	361
14 A Country Practice	Fri	535	14 Murphy Brown	Wed	341
15 Golden Fiddles	Sat	522	15 Bill	Tues	308
16 Naked Gun	Tues	521	16 Glenroe	Thurs	302
17 Flight of the Navigator	Fri	475	17 Oklahoma	Tues	300
18 Why Me?	Thurs	470	18 Perfect Strangers	Tues	295
19 1991 – A View	Thurs	470	19 Duel in The Sun	Sat	287
20 Play the Game	Sat	469	20 Eerie Indiana	Mon	240

The highest News rating in thousands, Friday: 992
The average News rating: 775

You will notice that the top seven choices on Network 2 were soap operas. The most popular programme on RTE 1 was also a soap—*Glenroe*.

*The letters TAM stand for Target Audience Measurement.

Soap Operas

What is it about soap operas which makes them such popular viewing?
Before looking in any detail at soap operas it might be interesting to learn
the origin of the expression.

The term 'soap opera' is an American one. It originally meant a radio or
television serial written to advertise certain products, usually soap powders,
which would be mentioned during the programme. The serial was paid for
by the advertisers. Nowadays, the term usually means any long-running serial.

Most British and Irish soap operas will have a number of common
characteristics:

1. On-going storyline.

2. Local settings.

3. Familiar characters who are realistic.

4. Themes arising out of domestic issues.

5. New characters are introduced infrequently.

The characteristics common to most American soaps are:

1. On-going storyline.

2. Glamorous settings.

3. Stereotyped* characters. The characters in American soaps tend to be either good or bad. There is usually a villain.

4. Themes arising out of love, sex, power, greed.

5. New characters are frequently introduced.

The characteristics common to many Australian soaps are:

1. On-going storyline.

2. Local settings.

3. Characters are unrealistic in that they sometimes appear to be too good to be true.

4. Issues are dealt with quite superficially.

5. New characters are regularly introduced.

The cast of *Neighbours* and *Home and Away* tend to be quite young which might account for their popularity with Irish teenagers.

*A stereotype is an over-simplified and fixed mental image of a person which is used or accepted by large numbers of people. The classes may be quite broad—Jews, white people, women, or much narrower—feminists, estate agents, rugby players. Stereotyping is normally accompanied by prejudice. Stereotyping people for whatever reason presents them as simpler, less individual and more predictable than they are.

We have pointed out the differences between Irish, American and Australian soap operas. However, they do have many characteristics in common. Two of the most obvious are:

1. In each episode there are a number of different storylines. Usually one major issue is dealt with and a number of minor issues are also pursued. These issues can continue over a number of episodes. The reason why there is a number of storylines in each episode is that if only one story was dealt with then only a few characters would be involved until that storyline was completed—this would be quite boring. Also, if a viewer missed a few episodes they would not feel that they had lost touch with what was happening. Some of the storylines might have been completed but the viewer would be familiar with some of the on-going issues. This is important as it makes the viewer feel involved.

2. Each episode ends on a 'cliff hanger'. The reason for this is obvious—it is to entice the viewer to watch the next episode—thus keeping up the TAM ratings!

Settings

Look at the characteristics common to the Irish and British soap operas. Why do you think that only a limited number of settings is used in each episode, e.g. home, café, shop, pub? Think about the 'wider' settings of these soaps:

Eastenders	—	square
Glenroe	—	farm/village
Coronation Street	—	street
Brookside	—	close/cul de sac
Fair City	—	street

Why do you think that producers have chosen these settings?

• List at least three advantages and three disadvantages of choosing one of these settings.

• Watch a few episodes of your favourite soap.

- Write your own episode introducing a *new character*. Remember that this should flow naturally from the existing storyline. You must make it clear where the character has come from and what connection s/he has with the village/square, etc.

This is a difficult exercise so perhaps it might be easier to work with a partner or in a small group. Your episode must be written in the form of a dialogue.

Obviously the producer does not want to pay too many salaries so now that you have introduced a new character, s/he might choose to get rid of an existing character. *You* must choose which character should go and how you should get rid of her/him. It is not acceptable to have the character walk in front of a bus or be beamed into outer space. Remember many viewers become quite attached to their 'soap families' so try to get rid of your character gently. Develop a strong and convincing storyline to explain the departure of your chosen character.

You may write up this exercise in the form of an extended memo to be presented by the producer at the weekly planning meeting.

Characters—Social Realism

Watch out for examples of stereotyping. Most of the characters in Irish and British soaps tend to be quite ordinary. Some are reasonably attractive; some are quite plain, unlike their American counterparts who are invariably beautiful, glamorous and wealthy. When we watch American soaps we are aware that we are entering a fantasy world. They tend to be sheer escapism. Whilst we watch them we can forget about our own problems. There is very little in an American soap to which we can actually relate. The stars of *Glenroe* and *Eastenders*, on the other hand, are ordinary working people whose problems are ones which we may have experienced ourselves.

Perhaps one of the reasons why British soaps such as *Eastenders* are so popular is because they portray lives which are infinitely worse than our own. We can watch them agonise over the difficulties of alcoholism, drug addiction, being unemployed or being a single parent. We can sympathise with them as some of us will have some of the same problems but few of us are likely to have quite so many. Think about Pauline Fowler and Dot Cotton—at the end of certain episodes we can heave a sigh of relief. In comparison to the bleakness of their lives, our own problems don't seem so bad!

Now is your big chance to break into the world of television. You have seen just how popular soap operas are so why not write your own? By now you should know all about the importance of the setting, the characters and the themes.

Develop an idea for a locally based soap opera. You may choose to set your soap opera in your school, in the estate on which you live or in your town or village.

Good luck and when you hit the big time, remember you read it here first!

Just suppose there was no more TV . . .

The most important thing we've learned,
So far as children are concerned,
Is never, NEVER, NEVER let
Them near your television set—
Or better still, just don't install
The idiotic thing at all.
In almost every house we've been,
We've watched them gaping at the screen.
They loll and slop and lounge about,
And stare until their eyes pop out.
(Last week in someone's place we saw)
A dozen eyeballs on the floor.)
They sit and stare and stare and sit
Until they're hypnotized by it,
Until they're absolutely drunk
With all that shocking ghastly junk.
Oh yes, we know it keeps them still,
They don't climb out the window sill,
They never fight or kick or punch,
They leave you free to cook the lunch
And wash the dishes in the sink—
But did you ever stop to think,
To wonder just exactly what
This does to your beloved tot?
IT ROTS THE SENSES IN THE HEAD!
IT KILLS IMAGINATION DEAD!
IT CLOGS AND CLUTTERS UP THE MIND!
IT MAKES A CHILD SO DULL AND BLIND
HE CAN NO LONGER UNDERSTAND
A FANTASY, A FAIRYLAND!
HIS BRAIN BECOMES AS SOFT AS CHEESE!
HIS POWERS OF THINKING RUST AND FREEZE!
HE CANNOT THINK— HE ONLY SEES!
'All right!' you'll cry, 'All right!' you'll
say,
'But if we take the set away,
What shall we do to entertain
Our darling children! Please explain!'
We'll answer this by asking you,
'What used the darling ones to do?
How used they keep themselves contented
Before this monster was invented?'

Have you forgotten? Don't you know?
We'll say it very loud and slow:
THEY . . . USED . . . TO . . . READ! They'd READ and READ,
AND READ and read, and then proceed
TO READ some more. Great Scott! Gadzooks!
One half their lives was reading books!
The nursery shelves held books galore!
Books cluttered up the nursery floor!
And in the bedroom, by the bed,
More books were waiting to be read!
Such wondrous, fine, fantastic tales
Of dragons, gypsies, queens, and whales
And treasure isles, and distant shores
Where smugglers rowed with muffled oars,
And pirates wearing purple pants,
And sailing ships and elephants,
And cannibals crouching round the pot,
Stirring away at something hot.

(It smells so good, what can it be?
Good gracious, it's Penelope.)
The younger ones had Beatrix Potter
With Mr Tod, the dirty rotter,
And Squirrel Nutkin, Pigling Bland,
And Mrs Tiggy-Winkle and—
Just How The Camel Got His Hump,
And How The Monkey Lost His Rump,
And Mr Toad, and bless my soul,
There's Mr Rat and Mr Mole—
Oh, books, what books they used to know,
Those children living long ago!
So please, oh please, we beg, we pray,
Go throw your TV set away,
And in its place you can install
A lovely bookshelf on the wall.
Then fill the shelves with lots of books,
Ignoring all the dirty looks,
The screams and yells, the bites and kicks,
And children hitting you with sticks—
Fear not, because we promise you
That, in about a week or two
Of having nothing else to do,
They'll now begin to feel the need
Of having something good to read.
And once they start—oh boy, oh boy!
You watch the slowly growing joy
That fills their hearts. They'll grow so keen
They'll wonder what they'd ever seen
In that ridiculous machine,
That nauseating, foul, unclean,
Repulsive television screen!
And later, each and every kid
Will love you more for what you did.

—**Roald Dahl**,
Charlie and the Chocolate Factory

Unit Two—Holidays

Summertime

What is summer? Well summer is...
> Arriving in a monsoon and being told by a sun-burnt courier
> 'Ah Señor! You should have been here last week.'
> A flooded tent site.
> Winter plus lawnmowing.
> Baggage-handlers' strikes.
> Getting delayed at an airport where the coffee machine doesn't take
> whatever currency you've changed your cheques into.
> Dead flies on your windscreen.
> Live flies on your sandwiches.
> Flying the Atlantic in five hours while your luggage flies the Pacific in six.
> Catching summer 'flu. And dysentery.
> Paying £5 for a strange drink that eats stomach linings.
> Getting the spot on the beach that turns out to be 'Hallelujah Corner'
> for an evangelist with a loudspeaker.
> The transistor in the next apartment that plays endless country-
> and-western in Serbo-Croatian.
> Long summer evenings.
> Wet long summer evenings.
> Trying to mime 'I demand to see the Consul' at a man with a funny
> uniform, a sabre scar, a jail—but no English.
> Trapped on a tourist bus driven by Enrico Kenival.*
> Finding your hotel is a two-hour climb, after you get off the burro's back.
> Being told that the funny-tasting sago was raw octopus spawn.
> Getting caught at Customs.
> Summer is all these things and more and we hope this magazine will
> help you appreciate some of its virtues and realise that the best laid
> plans of mice and travel agents 'gang aft a-gley'.
> Still it is the only summer we get, so we might as well enjoy it.

—Billy Simpson

*Probably better known as Evil Knievel.

(Billy Simpson might have avoided some of these problems if he had planned his holiday a little better.)

Stage One

In this unit you are organising your first independent holiday. Probably all your previous holidays have been family holidays—caravanning in West Cork or visiting relatives in England.

Before you decide where you would like to go and what you would like to do, you must think about how you will pay for the holiday—you may have a weekend job or possibly a regular baby-sitting job. Whatever way you intend raising the money, remember to avoid temptation. So don't keep your savings in a piggy bank, at home or in an old sock under your mattress. Open an account and make your money work for you. You may open an account with:

 *A bank*

 *A post office*

 *A credit union*

To decide which type of account you should open, you need to understand the following terms:

Deposit/Savings Account. If you want to save money, have your money secure and earn interest, this is probably the best account to open. When lodging money to a deposit account, a customer completes a lodgment slip. It is easy to withdraw money from a deposit account.

Current Account. People who wish to pay their bills by cheque often open a current account. Interest can be earned on money in some types of current accounts.

Cheque Book. A cheque has been defined as 'an unconditional order in writing to a bank, signed by the person giving it, requiring the bank to pay on demand, a sum of money to a specified person or the bearer of the cheque'. Cheques are issued by the banks in book form and have a standard layout.

Cheque Guarantee Card. These cards are given by the banks to their current account holders if the banks consider that they are creditworthy. The banks guarantee to honour the cheques up to a maximum of £100 for each cheque subject to all the conditions regarding the use of the cheque being met.

Automated Teller Machine (A.T.M.). Each bank has its own system. The main advantage of these machines is that they offer twenty-four-hour banking, seven days a week. The bank's customer is given a card. The customer uses this card, together with a secret code number, P.I.N. (Personal Identity Number) to withdraw cash. A customer may also deposit money with her/his card or order a bank statement.

Most banks have a Student Officer who would be happy to advise you. In your folder, draw up a list of the advantages and disadvantages of each type of account. Now decide which type of account you will choose. Fill in the appropriate application form which you have got from the bank/post office/credit union.

Your next step is to make your first deposit of money—**Lodgment**.

MEMORANDUM ONLY LODGMENT FOR CURRENT ACCOUNT	☘ Ulster Bank Limited	LODGMENT FOR CURRENT ACCOUNT Destination Branch Sort Code		£	p
A/c. _____ Date _____			Large Notes		
		Bank	£1 Notes		
Subject to Verification See conditions overleaf		ULSTER BANK LIMITED	50p Coin		
	Cashier's Stamp and Initials	Branch	Silver		
			Bronze		
Cashier's Stamp and Initials		Account in Name of	Total Cash		
	BA 152 (Rev. April 1980)		Cheques Etc. (see over)		
	Paid in by	Account Number	No. of Cheques and PO's		
£			£		

Now that you have taken your first step towards organising your holiday, the next decision must be—what kind of holiday do you want?

Stage Two

There are many different types of holiday available.

Beach holiday—

sea, sand, swimming, sun.

Activity holiday—

skiing, camel trekking, cycling,

mountaineering.

Cultural/archaeological—

cities, art galleries, museums,

Pyramids, theatre.

1. From the list below choose what would be most important to you.

Abseiling	Hillwalking
Cabaret	Swimming
Trains	Discos
Sand	Sailing
Food	Solitude
Sport	Skiing
Museums	Golf
Foreign places	Art galleries.

2. Working with a partner, imagine you are planning a holiday together. Compare your checklist and pick out those features which you have both chosen.

3. On the basis of this information and on how much money you think you can save you can now make a final decision on whether to holiday in Ireland or to travel abroad.

Whichever you decide on, it is always advisable to plan your holiday in advance.

You can have a wonderful holiday in Ireland even if you are on a very limited budget. So perhaps it would be a good idea to join the Irish Youth Hostel Association (I.Y.H.A.)/An Oige *or* the Youth Hostel Association of Northern Ireland (Y.H.A.N.I.). It would be also very wise to have an International Student Identity Card (I.S.I.C.) and/or a European Youth Card (E.Y.C.).

An Oige/I.Y.H.A.

An Oige was founded in 1931. The main aim of the organisation is to help all but especially the young, to an appreciation of the countryside. An Oige provides forty-seven youth hostels throughout Ireland. These youth hostels are part of a world-wide chain, numbering over 5,500 in all.

The great advantage of youth hostels is that they provide good, clean, inexpensive accommodation. They are usually situated in beautiful parts of the country—near beaches, mountains, lakes and rivers. This can give you an ideal base for an activity-based holiday, e.g. trekking, walking, cycling, mountaineering, water sports, etc.

For those of you who prefer to holiday in the city, there are also youth hostels in all the major cities.

Membership of An Oige not only provides you with economical accommodation but it also entitles you to avail of special train fares, special weekend breaks, group discounts and off-season discounts.

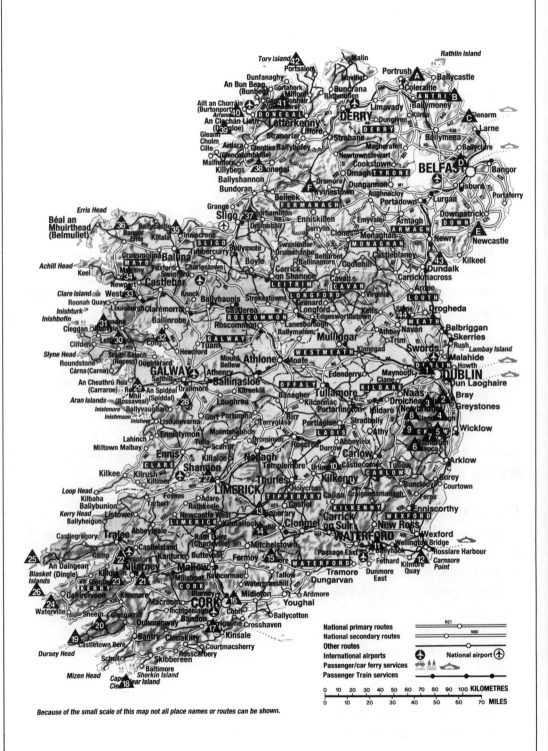

National primary routes
National secondary routes
Other routes
International airports
Passenger/car ferry services
Passenger Train services

National airport

Because of the small scale of this map not all place names or routes can be shown.

Irish Youth Hostel Association

SLIGO AND MELLIFONT YOUTH HOSTELS ARE NOW CLOSED
GALWAY INTERNATIONAL YOUTH HOSTEL, ST MARY'S COLLEGE,
ST MARY'S ROAD, GALWAY IS OPEN IN JULY AND AUGUST
-TEL (091) 27411 -FAX (091) 27410

Head Office
61 Mountjoy Street, Dublin 7.
Telephone: 353-1-304555.
Fax: 353-1-305808
Telex: 32988 IYHA.

DUBLIN

1. Dublin International Youth Hostel	Mountjoy Street, Dublin 7.	01-301766/301396	400	All Year
CO. WICKLOW				
2. Knockree	Enniskerry, Bray, Co. Wicklow	01-864036	56	All Year
3. Glencree	Enniskerry, Bray, Co. Wicklow	01-864037	40	All Year
4. Devil's Glen (Tiglin)	Ashford, Co. Wicklow	0404-40259	50	All Year
5. Glendalough	Glendalough, Co. Wicklow	0404-45342	80	All Year
6. Aghavannagh*	Aghavannagh Hse., Aughrim, Co. Wicklow	0402-36102	60	1/3-30/11
7. Glenmalure*	Greenane, Co. Wicklow	–	16	1/7-31/8
8. Blessington Lake (Baltyboys)*	Blessington, Co. Wicklow	045-67266	36	1/3-30/11
9. Ballinclea*	Donard, Co. Wicklow	045-54657	40	1/3-30/11
CO. KILKENNY				
10. Foulksrath Castle*	Jenkinstown, Co. Kilkenny	056-67674	54	1/3-31/10
CO. WEXFORD				
11. Arthurstown	Arthurstown, New Ross, Co. Wexford	051-89186	30	1/3-30/9
12. Rosslare	Rosslare Harbour, Co. Wexford	053-33399	85	All Year
CO. TIPPERARY				
13. Glen of Aherlow (Ballydavid Wood)*	Glen of Aherlow, Co. Tipperary	062-54148	40	1/3-30/11
14. Mountain Lodge	Burncourt, Cahir, Co. Tipperary	052-67277	30	1/3-30/9
CO. WATERFORD				
15. Lismore	Glengarra, Lismore, Co. Waterford	058-54390	36	1/4-30/9
CO. CORK				
16. Cork	1 Redclyffe, Western Rd., Cork	021-543289	110	All Year
17. Kinsale*	Summer Cove, Kinsale, Co. Cork	021-772309	48	1/3-31/12
18. Cape Clear Island	Cape Clear Island, Skibbereen, Co. Cork	028-39144	48	1/4-31/10
19. Allihies	Allihies, Bantry, Co. Cork	027-73014	34	1/4-30/9
CO. KERRY				
20. Glanmore Lake	Lauragh, Killarney, Co. Kerry	064-83181	36	1/4-30/9
21. Loo Bridge*	Clonkeen, Killarney, Co. Kerry	064-53002	30	1/3-30/9
22. Killarney	Aghadoe House, Killarney, Co. Kerry	064-31240/33355	220	All Year
23. Black Valley	Beaufort, Killarney, Co. Kerry	064-34712	50	All Year
24. Ballinskelligs	Ballinskelligs, Co. Kerry	0667-9229	24	All Year
25. Dun Chaoin - Dunquin	Dun Chaoin, Ballyferriter, Tralee, Co. Kerry	066-56121	60	All Year
26. Valentia Island	Knightstown, Valentia Island, Co. Kerry	0667-6154	40	1/4-30/9
CO. LIMERICK				
27. Limerick City	1, Pery Square, Limerick	061-314672	70	All Year
CO. GALWAY				
28. Burren (Doorus House)	Doorus House, Kinvara, Co. Galway	091-37173	56	All Year
29. Indreabhán	Indreabhán, Co. Galway	091-93154	66	All Year
30. Ben Lettery*	Ballinafad, Co. Galway	095-34636	52	All Year
31. Killary Harbour*	Rosroe, Renvyle, Co. Galway	095-43417	44	1/3-31/10
CO. MAYO				
32. Cong	Lisloughrey, Quay Road, Cong, Co. Mayo	092-46089	46	All Year
33. Westport	Altamount St., Westport, Co. Mayo	098-26644/26717	100	1/3-31/10
34. Traenlaur Lodge	Lough Feeagh, Newport, Co. Mayo	098-41358	32	All Year
35. Killala	Killala House, Killala, Co. Mayo	096-32172	50	All Year
36. Pollatomish	Pollatomish, Ballina, Co. Mayo	–	38	1/4-30/9
CO. SLIGO				
37. Sligo Town	Pearse Road, Sligo	071-43204	40	7/1-17/12
CO. DONEGAL				
38. Ball Hill	Donegal Town, Co. Donegal	073-21174	60	All Year
39. Crohy Head	Crohy Head, Dungloe, Co. Donegal	075-21330	36	1/4-31/10
40. Aranmore Island	Aranmore Island, Burtonport, Co. Donegal	–	33	1/5-30/9
41. Errigal*	Dunlewy, Gweedore, Co. Donegal	075-31180	46	All Year
42. Trá na Rosann	Downings, Co. Donegal	074-55374	40	All Year
CO. LOUTH				
43. Omeath*	Omeath, Dundalk, Co. Louth	042-75142	30	All Year
44. Mellifont	Collon, Drogheda, Co. Louth	041-26127	20	Closed for

alterations

27

YHANI (Youth Hostel Association of Northern Ireland)

56 Bradbury Place,
Belfast BT7 1RU.

Tel: (0232) 324733   Fax: (0232) 439699

Youth Hostel	Address	Telephone	Beds	Open
A. Whitepark Bay International	157 Whitepark Rd., Ballintoy, Ballycastle, Co. Antrim BT54 6NH	02657-31745	44	1/2-30/11
B. Cushendall	Layde Road, Cushendall, Co. Antrim BT44 0NQ	02667-71344	56	1/3-31/1
C. Ballygally	210 Coast Road, Ballygally, Co. Antrim BT40 2QQ	0574-583355	48	21/1-18/12
D. Belfast International	'Ardmore', 11 Saintfield Rd., Belfast BT8 4AE	0232-647865	60	7/1-19/12
E. Newcastle	30 Downs Road, Newcastle, Co. Down BT33 0AG	03967-22133	44+	1/2-31/12
F. Castle Archdale	Castle Archdale Country Park, Irvinestown, Co. Fermanagh BT94 1PP	03656-28118	44+	1/1-30/11

All Hostels may be booked in advance by groups throughout the year.
*These hostels remain open at weekends throughout the year. Enquire at head office about our Rent-a-Hostel Scheme.

AN OIGE MEMBERSHIP APPLICATION

39 Mountjoy Square, Dublin 1.
Telephone: (01) 363111/364750. Telex: 32988. Fax: 365807

Name: _____

Address: _____

_____

Telephone No: _____ Date of Birth: _____ Age Last Birthday: _____

Occupation: _____ Interests: _____

Were you a member last year? Yes ❑ No ❑

Are you interested in joining one of the groups with An Oige:

NEWCOMERS ❑   MOUNTAINEERING ❑   CYCLING ❑   PHOTOGRAPHIC ❑

Details from An Oige, 39 Mountjoy Square, Dublin 1.

Notes:
(i) Applicants are advised, membership is on a Calendar Year Basis. For Hostelling in Ireland the card is valid until the end of January in any year.
(ii) For applicants under 14 years of age: please have the following signed by your parent or guardian: **I am the parent (guardian) of the applicant and I am willing to allow him/her to be enrolled as Junior Member of An Oige.**

Signed: _____ Date: _____

Address: _____

(iii) Applicants are advised that detailed lists of An Oige activities including adventure weekends, holidays (at home and abroad) are published regularly by An Oige. Please contact head office for details.

Amount Enclosed £ _____

Declaration by Secondary School
To be completed by School Authorities

Name of student: _____

Name of school: _____

What class/year is the student attending? ____

Student's date of birth: _____

'I declare that the applicant named overleaf is a full-time student attending the above secondary school for a minimum of one academic year.'

School seal/stamp:

Official signature: _____

Eligibility and Conditions

Your International Student Identity Card is a personal document only, and is strictly non-transferable. The ISIC and Travelsave Stamp allow you to purchase one ticket per journey for your own use.

Your ISIC may be confiscated by any transport company for abuse of the ISIC or Travelsave scheme. In this case, a duplicate card will not be issued for a minimum of six months, and only subject to written application. Your name will be placed on a stoplist circulated to all issuing offices.

I declare that I am a full-time student and all the information on this form is true. I agree to abide by the conditions of the ISIC and Travelsave scheme above.

Signature: _____

 Use a dictionary to find out what is meant by the following words:

Non-transferable
Confiscated
Duplicate
Stoplist

Rewrite these words and their meanings into your folder.

Now that you have joined An Oige you decide to take an Easter Break: this is usually a good time to travel as the hostels will not be over-crowded.

Imagine that you have started your hostelling holiday in Kinsale, Co. Cork (Hostel No. 17). You have always wanted to visit the West of Ireland and the places which particularly interest you are:

Ballyvaughan, Co. Clare.

Westport, Co. Mayo.

Arranmore Island, Co. Donegal.

Gweedore, Co. Donegal.

Cushendall, Co. Antrim.

Plan your route carefully. Remember that you are travelling during April.

- Is it possible to stay overnight in all the places you would like to visit?

- You are on a limited budget so work out how much it will cost to stay overnight in each of the hostels.

- Unfortunately, the weather has been appalling. By the time you reach Co. Antrim you feel that though you have enjoyed your holiday you are now ready for a little pampering at your grandparents' home. They live in Kilkenny.

- Work out the quickest route from Cushendall to Kilkenny. You may use either bus or train services.

European Youth Card

The European Youth Card (E.Y.C.) is essential, whether you intend to holiday in Ireland or abroad. You do not have to be a student to benefit— everyone under twenty-six years of age is entitled to an E.Y.C. The E.Y.C. entitles you to discounts and benefits on cultural and sporting activities, commercial goods and services, as well as international travel benefits.

International Student Identity Card

The I.S.I.C. is recognised as proof of your student status and entitles the holder not only to travel discounts but also to cultural and retail discounts in more than fifty countries. With your I.S.I.C. you can get travel insurance, maps and guide books at special discounted rates.

For an extra £7 you can get a **Travelsave Stamp**. When you have this stamp on the back of your I.S.I.C., you are entitled to substantial discounts—sometimes up to 50%—on bus and rail networks.

APPLICATION FORM FOR I.S.I.C.

Surname

First name

Date of birth

Nationality

School/College name

Permanent address

Male ☐ Female ☐

Course of study/faculty

Is 1993/1994 your final year?   Yes ☐ No ☐

Did you have a 1992/1993 ISIC? Yes ☐ No ☐

If you do not wish to be include on USIT's mailing list please tick 'No' here.   No ☐

  Fill in this application form.

  What is meant by 'Mailing List'?

You might, however, decide with your friends to go abroad on your holiday. In order to choose your holiday destination, you should visit your local Travel Agent. Collect a number of brochures. Read them carefully, you will probably come across some words used in an unusual way.

Match the words in column 1 with the meaning in column 2. Do this exercise in your folder.

Courier	Money still owed after the deposit has been paid
Surcharge	Cost of meals and bedrooms
Package	Travel firm representative who helps out
Bed and breakfast	Extra payment
Supplement	Everything you have to pay for
Inclusive	Cost of bedroom and breakfast
Charter	Holiday where all travel, hotels, food etc. are paid for when booking
Itinerary	A trip
Departure	Extra payment for better accommodation
Deposit	An amount of money to confirm your booking
Balance	Details of holidays and excursions
Full Board	The time at which you must leave
Excursion	The travel company hires the means of transport

Now the time has come to *book* your holiday.

Remember you will be expected to pay a deposit. If you decide to cancel your holiday, your deposit will not be refunded. So be sure you choose wisely. Usually a deposit is 10% of the total cost. For example if your holiday—two weeks in the sun—costs £480, your deposit would be £48.

The balance (remainder) must be paid at least six weeks before departure. The balance can be paid by:

cheque money order
bank draft cash

Currently there is a £5 **Government Tax** (an exit levy), which must also be paid.

Travel Insurance. Although it is not compulsory, it is very sensible to take out Travel Insurance. This will protect you in the event of:

- sickness
- loss or theft of belongings
- accidents
- cancellation or curtailment of holiday

Form E111

It is worth remembering that Irish nationals can avail of public health facilities when visiting other EC countries by applying to their local Health Board for a **Form E111**.

Your Form E111 must be signed by a Health Officer. If you become ill or have an accident during your holiday, you are entitled to free medical and dental care, free medicines and hospitalisation. Form E111 only covers emergencies.

Stage Three

As this is your first holiday abroad, there are certain things which you may need:

 Passport

 Visa

 Vaccination

Passport. 'This is an official document showing identity and citizenship. It allows the person specified on it to travel to and from countries. It entitles the holder to protection.'

Application forms can be obtained from your local Garda Station.

ÉIRE   IRELAND

PASSPORT APPLICATION FORM

GENERAL

This form should be completed in block capitals using a ballpoint pen.

You should use this form only if you are resident in the State. Use PAS 2 form if you are resident outside the State.

To help you complete the application correctly you should first read the Explanatory Notes below. An Explanatory Note relating to each Section of the form is included, e.g Note 1 explains how to complete Section 1 of the form, Note 2 to complete Section 2 etc.

While applications are processed as quickly as possible **delays will arise** if documentation is not in order or if the application form is not completed fully and accurately. Please note that it takes a minimum of **two weeks** to process very urgent applications which are presented in person to the Passport Office. You should allow at least **four weeks** for the processing of your application during the non-peak season (1 October to 30 November each year) and **up to six weeks** during the remainder of the year.

Remember that you may need your passport some weeks prior to your travel date if you need to apply for a visa.

PASSPORTS FOR MINORS

Every citizen irrespective of age is entitled to an individual passport.

Children under 18 years may apply for a three year passport or a ten year passport—see Note 1. Parental consent, **PAS M,** signed by both parents or guardians, is required for each new passport.

Children under 16 years may be included on a parents passport and can travel **up to the age of 16** to most countries with the parent without separate passports. Parental consent, **PAS M,** signed by the other parent or guardian, is required—see Note 6.

PASSPORT PHOTOGRAPH REQUIREMENTS

—Two photographs, 35mm x 45mm
  Black line shows correct size
  Broken line shows smallest
  size acceptable

—Full face (without hat), head and shoulders only, against light background

—Thin photographic paper

—Reverse of photograph should be white and unglazed.

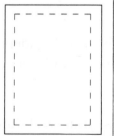

WARNING: A person who gives false information to get a passport or to help another person to get a passport may be prosecuted.

Explanatory Notes to help Applicants complete this Passport Application Form

Note 1 (Type of Passport Required)

Please note that it is not possible to renew or extend the validity of **any** passport. When the validity period of a passport expires a new passport will be required. Details of the type of passport you can apply for are given hereunder.

Standard Passport
A 32 page passport, valid for 10 years.

3 Year Passport—For persons under 18 years or over 65 years of age
A 32 page passport, valid for 3 years.

Large Passport
A 96 page passport, valid for 10 years, is available for persons who travel frequently and are likely to use up all the visa pages of a standard passport before the passport expires.

Replacement Passport
A Replacement (for either a Standard or a Large passport) may be obtained for the **unexpired period of validity of an existing one** provided the existing passport is not lost in which case a new one must be obtained. This type of passport may be applied for in the following situations:

—if all the visa pages are used up in the existing passport,

—if a name change is required to a passport (e.g on marriage etc.) or if applicant requires to add a child or children to the passport etc.

Parental consent is required in respect of any additional children being added to a replacement passport—see Note 6.

Lost/Mutilated Passports
A replacement cannot be issued if the original passport is lost or mutilated.

Reduced Low Season Fee for Standard Passports
In order to encourage applicants to apply for their passports outside of the peak season a reduced fee will apply to applications received from 1 October to 30 November for **standard passports**.

Fee Payment
Passport fees should be paid by cheque, postal order, money order or bank draft made payable to Passport Office. For security reasons **fees should not be paid by cash.**

Note 2 (Name)

Titles
Titles such as Mr, Mrs, Ms, Rev, Dr, Lord, Lady etc. are not entered on the passport.

Name to Appear on Passport
Applicants may have the **name they are normally known by** entered on the passport.

If the name to be entered on the passport is **different** from the name recorded in the birth certificate **evidence of usage** (for at least 2 years) must be submitted e.g bank statement, credit cards, driving licence, utility bills, school reports, etc. At least two such examples should be enclosed. In the case of married women the passport may be issued in the married name—production of a marriage certificate is sufficient.

Applicants are advised that difficulties may arise when application is being made for visas, work permits abroad etc. where the name on the passport **is not exactly the same** as that on the birth certificate, or as that on the marriage certificate, in the case of married women. To minimise these difficulties applicants (whose passport name differs from their birth certificate name) may choose to have their **birth certificate name** also entered on the observations page of the passport. To exercise this option applicants should put an 'X' in the **Yes** box in Section 2 of the application form.

Name on Birth Certificate
This part of Section 2 need only be completed if the **birth certificate name** differs from the **name to appear on passport.**

Note 3 (Personal Information).

Place of Birth: Enter **County** of birth if you were born in Ireland or **Country,** if born abroad.

Present address: This is the address to which your Passport will be posted.

Home Address: If your present address is a temporary one, enter your home address here, otherwise leave blank.

Signature of Applicant: This should reflect the 'Name to appear on Passport' e.g if name to appear on passport is Pat Murphy signature should either be Pat Murphy or P Murphy, **not** Patrick or Paddy Murphy.

You should sign the application form **twice** in the space and within the lines provided.

Telephone: Give both your **Home** and **Work** phone numbers including the **Area Code.**

Note 4 (Previous Irish Passports)

Ensure that you record on the application form the number of your most recent Irish passport and submit it for cancellation. If it has been lost or was stolen a Statement of Loss (on form **PAS L**) must be completed, witnessed at a Garda Station and submitted with your application. There is no need to submit passports which have already been cancelled by the Passport Office.

Note 5 (Citizenship).

Only Irish citizens may obtain an Irish passport.

To prevent potential fraud all applications for passports must be supported by an original long form birth certificate and any previously issued passport which has not yet been cancelled by the Passport Office.

Documentary evidence **(original certificates only)** in the following form must be provided to confirm your entitlement to Irish citizenship:

If born in Ireland
— your long form birth certificate (not photocopy and not baptismal certificate), and
— any previously uncancelled Irish passport.

If born outside Ireland to an Irish-born parent
— your long form or vault copy birth certificate,
— Irish parent's long form birth certificate,
— parents' marriage certificate, and
— any previously uncancelled Irish passport.

If you have acquired Irish citizenship by Naturalisation, Foreign Births Registration (FBR) or Post Nuptial Declaration
— documentary evidence of citizenship (original documents only) e.g Naturalisation Certificate, FBR Certificate, letter of acceptance of your Post Nuptial Citizenship,
— your long form or vault copy birth certificate,
— any previously uncancelled Irish passport, and
— an authenticated translation of all certificates is required if they are not in English.

If you have been adopted under Irish law,
— your long form birth certificate, and
— long form birth certificate of adoptive parent who is an Irish citizen.

Note 6 (Your Children under 16 years)

Children under 16 years named on your passport may normally travel with you without separate passports. To include children on your passport please:
— complete the details required at Section 6 of the application form,
— provide the witnessed consent **of the other parent or guardian** by completing and enclosing the **PAS M** form,
— enclose the **long form birth certificate** for each child you wish to put on your passport, and
— if the guardianship of the child/children is the subject of a separation agreement or court order, include all relevant legal documents—original documents.

PAS 1

Note 7 (Declaration by Applicant)

Please note that this Declaration should be signed by you in a Garda Station in the presence of member of the Garda Síochána and should be submitted to the Passport Office **within 6 months** of the date on which the declaration was witnessed.

Note 8 (Certificate of Identity)

This Section should be completed at a Garda Station by a member of the Garda Síochána who should:

— satisfy her/himself as to your identity and that the photographs supplied are a true likeness of you.

— ensure that you sign Section 7 of form in her/his presence

— sign, date and complete Section 8 of the application form and sign the back of the photographs supplied by you.

CHECK LIST ON ITEMS TO ACCOMPANY THE COMPLETED APPLICATION FORM

Please ensure that,

(a) **the application form** is completed fully and accurately in Block Capitals using a ballpoint pen.

(b) you have signed the form **in the presence of a member of the Garda Síochána** (see Note 7).

(c) that you have enclosed the following items with your application

— **photographs (35mm x 45mm)**—two recent identical passport photographs signed on the back by the witness—see diagram,

— the **correct fee**—see Note 1 and Section 1,

— your most recent previous **Irish passport**—see Note 4, and

— all necessary **documents/certificates, originals only**—see Note 5 and, where applicable, see Notes 2 and 6 and the heading 'Passports for Minors'.

Please send completed application to:

Passport Office,   or   Passport Office,
Molesworth Street,   Irish Life Building,
Dublin 2.   1a South Mall, Cork.
(01) 711633   (021) 272525/276964.
Office hours: 9.30 – 4.30   9.30 – 12.30
   1.30 – 4.00

PAS 1 — Passport Application Form

For Official Use Only

Post/Counter/D.O.....................................

O of R..   Checked by (Ctr)....................................

O of I..   Checked by (Sn)....................................

Date Rec'd..   OK'd for issue by...................................

Atp..............................   ....   Calling Y/N DPR.....................................

Passport No..................................... Date of Issue................................... Date of Expiry...............................

SECTION 1 TYPE OF PASSPORT REQUIRED (See Note 1)

(Put an 'X' in appropriate boxes)

Standard IR£45　　　　　(1) ☐　(Applies to applications received from 1 December to 30 September)

Standard Low Season IR£35 (2) ☐　(Applies to applications received from 1 October to 30 November)

3 Year IR£10　　　　　(3) ☐　(Applies to applications received for persons under 18 and over 65 only)

Large IR£90　　　　　(4) ☐

Replacement Passports:　　Standard for Standard IR£15　(5) ☐　　Large for Large IR£27　(6) ☐

Payment Type: Cheque (1) ☐　　Money Order (2) ☐　　Bank Draft (4) ☐　**NB: Fees should not be paid by cash.**

　　　　　　　　　　　　Postal Order (3) ☐　　_____ (5) ☐

SECTION 2 NAME (See Note 2)

NAME TO APPEAR ON PASSPORT

Surname ☐☐☐☐☐☐☐☐☐☐☐☐☐☐☐☐☐☐☐☐☐☐☐☐

Forename 1 ☐☐☐☐☐☐☐☐☐☐☐☐☐☐☐☐

Forename 2 ☐☐☐☐☐☐☐☐☐☐☐☐☐☐☐☐

NAME ON BIRTH CERTIFICATE
(Complete this part of Section 2 **only** if name to appear on passport differs from **birth certificate name).**

Surname ☐☐☐☐☐☐☐☐☐☐☐☐☐☐☐☐☐☐☐☐☐☐☐☐

Forename 1 ☐☐☐☐☐☐☐☐☐☐☐☐☐☐☐☐

Forename 2 ☐☐☐☐☐☐☐☐☐☐☐☐☐☐☐☐

Do you wish to have your birth certificate name recorded in passport? (See Note 2, fourth paragraph)

　　　　　Yes ☐　　　　　　No ☐　　　**(Put an 'X' in appropriate box)**

SECTION 3 PERSONAL INFORMATION (See Note 3)

　　　　　　　Day Month Year　　　　　　　County (or Country if born abroad)　　Male Female

Date of Birth: ☐☐☐　*Place of Birth:* _____　*Sex:* ☐　☐

e.g. if 3 March 1950
write 03 03 50　　　　　　　　　　　　　　　　　　　　　　**(Put an 'X' in appropriate box)**

Present Address:
(to which passport
will be sent)

　　　　　　　　　　　　　　　　　Home Address

Your Normal
Signature Twice　　　_____
(See Note 3)　(1)
(within lines)　　　_____
at 1 and 2　(2)

　　　　　　　　　_____

Telephone: (Including Area Code) [_____]　Home　[_____]　Business

SECTION 4   PREVIOUS IRISH PASSPORT (See Note 4)

Were you ever issued with an Irish Passport?   Yes ☐   No ☐   **(Put an 'X' in appropriate box)**

If yes, submit your most recent Irish passport for cancellation and quote the passport number. ☐☐☐☐☐☐☐☐☐

If you are not in a position to do so submit a detailed explanation and statement of loss (form **PAS L**) witnessed by a member of the Garda Síochána.

SECTION 5   CITIZENSHIP (See Note 5)

Please indicate citizenship category to which you belong: **(Put an 'X' in appropriate boxes)**

1.   Irish born   (1)   ☐

If you were born in Northern Ireland since 6 December 1922 answer questions at (a) to (c) below.

		Yes	No
(a)	Have you (or a parent or a grandparent of yours, born in Ireland) ever had an Irish passport?	☐	☐
(b)	Was any one of your parents or grandparents born in any part of Ireland before 6 December 1922, or in the State (26 counties) on or after that date?	☐	☐
(c)	Could any parent or grandparent of yours, born in Northern Ireland, have answered 'Yes' to question (b) above?	☐	☐

If you cannot answer 'Yes' to any of the above questions, you should ask for a separate form on which you can declare that you are an Irish citizen.

2.   Born abroad of an Irish-born parent   (2)   ☐   Enclose birth and marriage certificates of Irish-born parent.

Indicate birth certificate name of Irish parent _____ and Date and

Place of Birth of that parent _____

3.   Naturalisation   (3)   ☐   FBR   (4)   ☐   Post Nuptial   (5)   ☐   Irish Adoption   (6)   ☐

SECTION 6   YOUR CHILDREN UNDER 16 YEARS (See Note 6)

	BIRTH CERTIFICATE NAME	Date of Birth	Sex	PLACE OF BIRTH (See Note 3) County (or country)
Surname	Forenames			
1				
2				
3				
4				
5				
6				

NB: If name to appear on passport differs from birth certificate name give details hereunder or on a separate sheet and evidence of usage. (See Note 2).

1 _____   4 _____

2 _____   5 _____

3 _____   6 _____

Do you wish to have the birth certificate name(s) recorded in passport? (See Note 2, fourth paragraph)

Yes ☐   No ☐   **(Put an 'X' in appropriate box)**

SECTION 7   DECLARATION BY APPLICANT (See Note 7)

Please sign in a Garda Station in the presence of a Garda.
I declare that the particulars in this application are correct, that the accompanying certificates relate to me (and my child/children) and that the accompanying photographs are of me.

Signature of applicant_____

If applicant is unable to sign, a parent/guardian should sign here_____

SECTION 8   CERTIFICATE OF IDENTITY (See Note 8)

Please have this Section completed at a Garda Station by a member of the Garda Síochána.
I certify that I have satisfied myself as to the identity of the applicant who has signed Section 7 above in my presence. I also certify that the photographs (on the back of which I have signed my name) supplied with this application are a true likeness of the applicant.

Signature of Garda _____

Name (in block letters) _____

Rank _____

Garda Number_____   Date_____

Garda Station _____

Telephone Number (including Area Code) _____

STATION STAMP

To apply for a passport you need:

- A copy of your Birth Certificate

- Two photographs

- £45—either cheque, postal order or bank draft.

During peak holiday time, the Passport Office will be particularly busy, so apply well in advance.

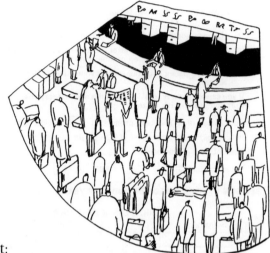

As part of this assignment you must:

- Complete a Passport Application Form

- Find out where your Birth Certificate may be obtained.

Visa. A visa is a special stamp on a passport showing that the passport has been found correct. It allows the holder to enter or leave a country. For travel to most European countries, a visa is not required. If you wish to travel to America or Australia, you must have a visa.

Vaccination. Vaccination has been defined as inoculating with vaccine to procure immunity from smallpox or with vaccine of any disease in order to produce it in mild form and so prevent a serious attack.

Using your dictionary, find out the meaning of the following words:

Inoculate

Procure

Immunity

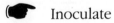 Write down these definitions in your folder.

Your local doctor would be furious if twenty-five of you stormed her/his surgery all looking for the same information. As part of this assignment, make a decision within the group as to which person should find out from the doctor all the details regarding vaccination. These should include:

- Cost

- When the vaccine should be administered

- Possible side-effects

- How one proves that s/he has been vaccinated.

Stage Four

Foreign Currency

When you travel abroad you cannot take your Irish money and use it in another country. You must use that country's own currency. To avoid carrying large amounts of cash, most people take **Eurocheques** or **Traveller's Cheques**—which they can exchange for the local currency. Find out what currency is used in the country you are planning to visit.

Below are two columns; match up each country with its currency. Write the correct pairs into your folder.

Austria	Lira
England	Pesetas
France	Guilders
Germany	Kroner
Holland	Francs
Italy	Deutschmarks
Norway	Drachmas
Spain	Pounds Sterling
Greece	Schillings

Convert IR£100 into each of the above currencies. Check the national newspapers or banks for up-to-date exchange rates.

 Copy this map of Europe into your folder. Write the name of each country and its currency into its correct space on the map.

When you travel abroad, you will discover that each country has its own culture, traditions and language. These should be respected. Many things will be strange to you, so perhaps it would be wise to stock up on some items with familiar brand names before you leave home, e.g. sickness tablets, sun lotions, camera, films etc.

Although no one expects you to be able to speak the language of the country you are visiting, most people appreciate it if you make the effort to learn a few phrases. Simple phrase books are readily available.

Remember, being on holiday is an adventure—so *be adventurous*. Perhaps the thought of eating snails fills you with horror and as for the idea of guinea pig with chocolate sauce—words may fail you. However, don't dismiss the local cuisine.

Bon Voyage!

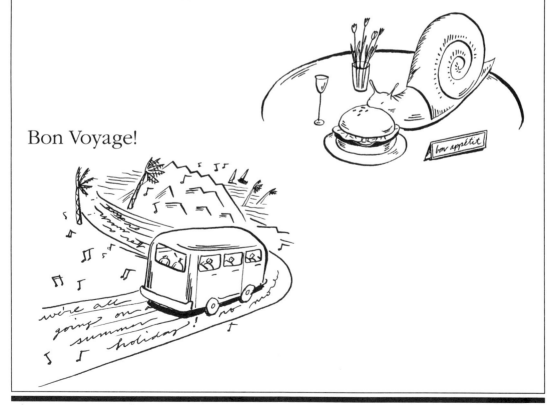

Unit Three—Mind Your Own Business

'Who wants to be a millionaire?'—'I Do'

Working through this unit should help you to learn all you need to know about setting up your own business, and perhaps in the future you will be able to put the skills learned here into practice.

No doubt you have all heard of companies like Jefferson Smurfit, Dunnes Stores, Cement Roadstone and Ballygowan. It is unlikely that your venture into the world of business will trouble these companies or cause alarm on the Stock Exchange. Remember, however, that these companies also had to start from an original idea. The first and most important rule in business is to have an idea, to think big but to start small.

Your school-based business enterprise will operate along the same lines as a multi-national company—except on a far smaller scale. For your enterprise to be successful your whole class must be involved. Decisions must be made democratically. Further on in this unit the structure of a school enterprise/company will be explained. Decisions can then be made about allocating jobs to each person according to their talents.

Your first task is to approach one of your teachers and ask her/him to be your advisor/co-ordinator. Remember—this is your company and you should not expect or want your teacher to take charge. Your next activity is to organise a formal meeting of your class group. At this meeting the following matters must be discussed:

1. Objectives

2. Possible services/products

3. Capital

4. Market research

At every formal meeting a record must be kept. These records are called **Minutes**. Minutes are a brief written record of a meeting noting the discussion which took place and the decisions which were reached.

Sample Agenda

A meeting will be held

on Wednesday 10 November 1993

at 11.30 a.m. sharp

in Room 6.

Re: **Formation of Mini-Company**

> **AGENDA**
>
> 1. Objectives
>
> 2. Possible Services/Products
>
> 3. Capital
>
> 4. Marketing Research
>
> 5. A.O.B.*

* A.O.B. means 'Any Other Business'

It is too early yet to elect a permanent secretary but someone in your group must take the role of acting secretary for this first meeting. The secretary's duties are:

• To keep minutes of every meeting.

• To send out letters and reports where necessary.

• To write up the **Agenda**—this is a list of items of business to be considered/discussed at a meeting.

As your company is democratic and non sexist, there is absolutely no reason why—in a mixed group—the secretary should automatically be female.

Objectives

The obvious objective of any company/business is to make a profit. In business when you have paid all your outgoings—the cost of making the product, advertising, wages etc.—the money that is left over is called profit.

If, after you have paid all your outgoings, there is no money left over, this is known in business as 'breaking even'. As you can imagine this is not a satisfactory state of affairs. However, if you are unable to pay your outgoings your company is operating at a loss. This is a disastrous state of affairs.

Another objective is to acquire the skills necessary to run a successful company. These skills include:

- Making decisions

- Communicating ideas

- Learning to work as part of a team.

Possible Products/Services

You must be realistic in your choice of product or service for your enterprise. Make sure you have access to the necessary equipment, machinery, utensils, etc.

You might like to consider the following:

- Organising a car wash/wax/valeting service.

- Running a school tuck shop, supplying your own cakes, sandwiches and snacks.

- Preparing and serving meals for the staff of your school (take-away orders also).

- Making soft toys/crafts, selling them at Christmas-time or perhaps organising a school fair at which to sell them.

- Producing Christmas tree stands and other seasonal decorations.

- If your school is lucky enough to have a pottery department, you could produce and sell a range of household pottery.

- Designing and producing your own range of Christmas, birthday and invitation cards.

- Creating a range of woodwork/metalwork goods—book-shelves, coffee tables, mug trees, video racks, etc.

- Designing and producing candles.

- Making tablecloths, napkins, etc.

Banks—Small Businesses

Many banks have a special advisory service to help people who are planning to set up their own businesses. Perhaps you could contact one of the local banks and see whether their small business advisor would come in and talk to you.

Your first exercise in this unit is to write a letter to the Principal of your school outlining your plans.

- Ask the Principal for permission to set up your student enterprise/mini company.

- Tell the Principal that a teacher has agreed to act as advisor/co-ordinator.

- In particular, ask whether the school's insurance is adequate.

Remember, your letter should be carefully thought out and concise. If the Principal seeks further information, you must present all the relevant information in a business-like fashion.

Capital

To start your company, you need money. This is known as capital. As you are not a charity, people will not give you money for your company unless they can expect to benefit. Money/capital is raised by the sale of **shares**.

A share is one of the equal parts into which a company's capital is divided. Every shareholder is entitled to a share of the profits. Each shareholder is given a **Share Certificate**.

____ 'shares' (limit five shares)	SHARE CERTIFICATE NON TRANSFERABLE
AMBER CATERING COMPANY	**AMBER CATERING COMPANY**
THIS IS TO CERTIFY that Ms Mr _____ (full name in capitals of _____ _____ (full address in capitals)	THIS IS TO CERTIFY that Ms Mr _____ (full name in capitals of _____ _____ (full address in capitals)
is the owner of ____ 'shares' par value of £1.00 each, in the above mentioned company. For each such 'share' the sum of £1.00 has been paid.	is the owner of ____ 'shares' par value of £1.00 each, in the above mentioned company. For each such 'share' the sum of £1.00 has been paid.
Given this _____day of ____199___	Given this _____ day of _____ 199___
_____Co-ordinator _____General Manager _____Date Date to be entered in Share Register by secretary.	_____Co-ordinator _____ Director

Hopefully, your company is going to make so much money that people will be queuing frantically to buy shares. Sadly, you must disappoint them because you are only allowed to sell a limited number of shares. Once you have decided on your enterprise you will have some idea of how much money you will need. You should not exceed £100.

As it is your company you will want to buy a share in it—if you don't have confidence in the product/service you are offering you can't reasonably expect others to. Once you have bought a share in your company you become a Director. As a Director you are entitled to sit on the Board of Directors and to run the company. Your other duty is to look after the interests of the other shareholders.

You may only sell shares to the teachers in your school and to members of your family. Each person may only buy a limited number of shares. The Board of Directors will set this limit.

Market Research

There is absolutely no point in setting up a business if there is not a market for the product/service you intend to offer. You have already discussed a number of possibilities; now you need to find out which will make you the most money.

How do you do this?

You ask people which product/service would appeal to them; what price would they be prepared to pay.

This is known as Market Research.

You should not ask vague open-ended questions. You must be specific. You are looking for definite information, therefore, you must ask definite questions.

Organise a meeting during which you should compile a questionnaire. You should deal with the following:

1. Product

2. Price

3. Whether product/service should be offered on a daily/weekly/monthly basis.

4. Distribution—should your customers come to you or should you deliver?

Before the close of this meeting, you should write up your questionnaire neatly. You should carry out the Market Research before the next meeting.

Your next task is to approach your Target Group and ask the questions. This is not as easy as it sounds. Many people are reluctant to answer questions and may feel embarrassed. You must, at all times, be courteous, even if people are rude to you. If someone refuses to answer your questions—don't persist, just walk away. Ask your questions clearly and distinctly and record the answers. When you have completed your questionnaires:

- Write a **report** of your findings and present it to your next group meeting. (See **Report Writing**, Unit 11, page 178)

- It might be helpful to use graphs. This visual aid can make a great impact. No doubt your Maths teacher will be delighted to help here.

- Finally, you must arrange a date, time and place for your next meeting.

This next meeting will be very important because the following matters will be dealt with:

1. Choice of name for the company

2. Advertising

3. Personnel

4. Any other business.

Choice of Name for the Company

'What's in a name? That which we call a rose by any other name would smell as sweet.'

Shakespeare—*Romeo and Juliet*

It is very important that the name you select for your enterprise should be apt, clever and reflect the nature of your business. In our unit on motoring, we mention a driving school in London called 'The Impact School of Motoring'. We ask you if this is an appropriate name. Do you think that a catering company called 'Burnt Offerings' would appeal to the lover of good food? Remember yours is a democratic company, so you should vote on the final choice of name.

Advertising

You are no doubt all familiar with the old saying—'It pays to advertise'— and indeed it does. The object of all product advertising is to sell the product.

Your next task is to design an advertisement/poster for your product. Your advertisement should be:

Eyecatching —Think about your Target Audience. Design your poster with them in mind.

Informative —Your advertisement must give all details of the service/product offered, prices and where this service/product is available.

The company name and logo should be displayed prominently on the advertisement.

Poster

You must also decide where to display your advertisements. Obviously, there is no point in displaying your advertisement behind the door of the boiler room. Choose areas where your poster will receive maximum exposure—school entrance, canteen, library, etc.

Personnel

Every company needs a proper working structure, otherwise there would be chaos. Although your company is run on democratic lines, it must have a correct structure. It doesn't matter what your role or title is, *each* job within the company has equal importance.

As it is your company, and you have bought a share in it, you are now called a **Director**. As a group, you are called the **Board of Directors**.

The duties of the Board of Directors are:

- To look after the interests of the shareholders.
- To see that the company acts within the law.
- To decide on policy.
- To be responsible for the production of a satisfactory and profitable product.

Meetings would be too clumsy and chaotic if all the Directors were to attempt to speak at once. To avoid this, the Board of Directors appoint a **General Manager** who will also act as **Chairperson**.

- It is the Chairperson who controls the meeting.
- The Chairperson will ensure that all items on the agenda are discussed.
- The Chairperson should make sure that no one person monopolises the meeting.

- When you wish to speak at a meeting, you ask the Chairperson's permission—this is known as 'speaking through the Chair'.

As meetings may become unruly and heated at times, it is important that the person you elect should be calm and clear thinking. It is the Chairperson's job to see that all items on the agenda are discussed in the order in which they appear on the agenda. You may, for example, be longing to discuss Item 4 but you must wait until the other items have been dealt with.

Production Manager. It is the job of the Production Manager to oversee the development of the product from start to finish. S/he is responsible for checking the quality of the product and ensuring that the product reaches the customer by the agreed date. The person you elect as Production Manager should:

- Be methodical in her/his approach to work

- Not panic when things go wrong

- Be logical in searching for a solution to a problem.

A calm person is the obvious choice.

Finance Officer.   The job of Finance Officer is to keep careful and accurate account of monies received and monies spent. These accounts should be kept in separate ledgers. A ledger is a special book for keeping accounts. Your commerce teacher would be happy to help you.

Accounts should be available for inspection. Because this money is not your own it is essential that you can account for every penny. The person you elect for this job should be good with money and should be neat and methodical in her/his presentation of work.

Sales Manager.   It is the job of the Sales Manager to achieve good sales for your product. It is easy to sell a product if someone wants to buy it, however the real skill lies in persuading a person who has no interest in your product that it is exactly what they need. The person you elect for this job should be outgoing, articulate, pleasant and be able to get on well with people.

Advertising Manager. The job of the Advertising Manager is to promote your product to the public. Although you have already designed a poster for this unit, it is the Advertising Manager who will have the final say about which posters should be used as part of your advertising campaign. It is also the job of the Advertising Manager to ensure that any posters which have been defaced or removed should be replaced.

The Target Group should not be allowed forget the existence of your product. The person you elect to this position should be good at art, creative and imaginative.

Secretary. The duties of the secretary have been dealt with elsewhere in this unit. The person you elect to this position should be reliable, able to express her/himself clearly and write legibly.

Before electing officers you should know the procedure which you must follow.

- First, draw up a list of positions to be filled.
  Remember, you want the most suitable person for the job, so don't automatically suggest your best friend. Don't forget you are in business to make money.

- Draw up a list of nominations.

These are the names of people who are thought to be most suitable for the job. The person who suggests the name is called the **Nominator** or the **Proposer**. A second person must support the nomination. This person is called the **Seconder** i.e. s/he 'seconds the nominations'.

If only one person is nominated and seconded for a position then that person is elected unopposed. If, however, there are two or more nominations, the group must decide by means of a vote. This can be done either through a 'show of hands' or by drawing up a ballot paper and voting for the person of your choice.

Before bringing this meeting to a close, it is the job of the newly elected General Manager/Chairperson to arrange the date and time for your next meeting.

Every company must hold an **Annual General Meeting** (A.G.M.) to which all shareholders may be invited. At this meeting each elected officer will present a report about their own particular area of responsibility.

As this is a class project your business will obviously have a limited lifespan. Before winding up your business you must present all reports, and then—the moment you have all been waiting for—you will share out the profits. This means that each shareholder will get back their original investment plus their share of the profits. This is known as the **dividend**.

You may think that only the most intelligent of people can set up and run their own business. This is not true. In the world of business there are thousands of people with few academic qualifications. Many even left school at an early age yet they have managed to make it to the top. Common sense, hard work and instinct are important ingredients in success.

Read the 'Hot Dog Story'—it proves the point. Remember also the famous words of Thomas Edison who said—'Genius is one per cent inspiration and ninety-nine per cent perspiration.'

Good Luck

The Hot Dog Story

A man lived by the side of the road and sold hot dogs.

He was hard of hearing so he had no radio.

He had trouble with his eyes so he read no newspapers.

But he sold good hot dogs.

He put up a sign on the highway telling how good they were.

He stood at the side of the road and cried 'Buy a hot dog Mister'.

And people bought.

He increased his meat order and bun orders.

He bought a bigger stove to take care of his trade.

He got his son home from college to help.

But then something happened . . .

His son said: 'Father haven't you heard the news?

There's a big recession on.

The unemployment situation is terrible.

The energy situation is worse'.

Whereupon the father thought 'Well my son has been to college he reads the papers and listens to the radio, and he ought to know'.

So his father cut down on his meat and bun order.

Took down his advertising signs.

And no longer bothered to stand on the highway to sell hot dogs.

And his hot dog sales fell almost overnight.

'You're right son' the father said to the boy.

'We are certainly in the middle of a great recession'.

(*The Manager*, March 1992)

Unit Four—Fundraising

Within this unit, there are a number of tasks which must be completed. The unit involves the organisation of a fundraising event.

Remember to keep a copy in your folder of all the letters you write and any speeches you prepare.

Every year there are many appeals for money to help the victims of famine, natural disasters and wars. It is often financially difficult to respond to all these appeals. However, the Irish are noted for their generosity. Perhaps one reason for this could be the fact that the Irish have a history and memory of their own famine of 1848. We have all been shocked by the disturbingly graphic pictures of dying children and resigned and starving adults which we have seen on television. To raise money for these victims, people have organised sponsored walks, fasts, parachute jumps and street collections. Perhaps you have taken part in such an event?

For the purpose of this assignment, you have decided to organise a fundraising event—a disco/dance. Choose the charity which you would like to support.

To make sure that the disco is a success, there are a number of stages which must be completed. Obviously, you will be working as part of a group but, depending on your individual skills, you will choose specific areas of responsibility.

It is important to remember that decisions within the group should be made democratically. Decisions should not be monopolised by the most vocal member of the group.

Stage One

Decide on your choice of venue—either the school hall or the youth club.
Having made the decision, you must now contact the person in charge.
Write a formal letter asking whether you may use the hall, asking for an
early reply and enquiring about the insurance cover. You may use the
sample layout below as a guide.

1. | YOUR ADDRESS |

2. | DATE |

3. | SCHOOL/YOUTH CLUB ADDRESS |

4. | GREETING
DEAR SIR/MADAM/MR O'SHEA/MS O'HALLORAN |

5. | Explain the reason why you
would like to use the hall. |

6. | Enquire about insurance
cover i.e. public liability. |

7. | Request an immediate reply. |

8. | Yours faithfully/sincerely
Signature. |

You use 'Yours sincerely' if you know the name of the person to whom you are writing and 'Yours faithfully' if you have used 'Dear Sir/Madam'.

You have been given permission to use the school hall or youth club. Now approach your head teacher, tell her/him about your plan and ask to borrow £20 to be used as a 'float'. It is very important that a careful account should be kept of all expenses and all receipts should be retained. Before you make any other plans, write a letter to confirm your acceptance of the use of the hall. To avoid any possible confusion, be very clear about the date and times of your booking.

Stage Two

Live Music or Disc Jockey?

In your folder, list the advantages and disadvantages of having either a live band or disc jockey. Use the points you have made to reach a decision.

Write to the DJ/band you have picked. Book them for the disco. Perhaps you could seek a reduction in the fee as your event is for charity.

Your disco is obviously going to be so popular that everyone will want to attend. This could be a problem as space is limited. To avoid a crush on the night, you should decide now whether you will restrict entrance to those who buy their tickets in advance or whether you will operate on a first come, first served basis. List in your folder the advantages and disadvantages of both methods.

Supervision

To ensure that everyone enjoys the disco and that everyone is safe, there should be adequate adult supervision. Perhaps your teachers, parents, youth leaders would be willing to help. An informal, polite request would be sufficient.

Maybe you feel you would not need adult supervision at the disco.

- Why do you think that adults would insist on adult supervision?

- Can you make a convincing case why there should not be adult supervision at a youth disco?

- Prepare your argument in advance and then formally debate the issue.

Stage Three

Publicity

Design a poster advertising the disco. It is important that your poster should be:

- Eye-catching

- Brief

- Contain all relevant information.

Perhaps the art department in your school would be prepared to help you. The group must decide where the posters should be placed to achieve maximum exposure.

Local Radio   As your disco is for charity, your local radio would be willing to publicise the event. Remember that local radio reaches the parts other media cannot!

You have been asked to give a brief talk about your fundraising activity. State the reasons why you are organising the event and why people should support it.

It is important to:

- Speak clearly
- Speak slowly
- Vary the tone of your voice

'Um', 'Er', and 'Like you know' are banned. They serve no useful purpose. You should each deliver your talk to the class and, on the basis of this oral presentation, you should decide who should speak on the local radio. Everyone should tape her/his speech. It may prove quite a shock when you hear yourself on tape!

Raffle and Spot Prizes

Using the Golden Pages telephone directory, make a list of local businesses, shops and companies.

- Write a letter requesting either money or gifts which could be used as raffle/spot prizes. Phrase your letter as a request, not a demand.

- Allow a few days for the letter to arrive, then follow up the letter with a telephone call.

- Before making your telephone call, decide what you are going to say.

Stage Four

Accounting and Banking

You have already kept careful account of any money you have spent from your original £20 float. It might be a good idea to buy a small accounts book in which you can record all your expenses. Remember, keep all your receipts and keep a record of any telephone calls you have made. Remember, this £20 must be repaid. Your accounts should be available for inspection.

Now that the disco is over, the proceeds must be sorted and counted before being lodged in the bank. Looking after a large amount of money, especially when it is not your own, is a very serious responsibility. Make sure that the money is kept securely overnight.

Contact the charity you have been supporting and let them know how much money you have raised.

You have worked very hard, you deserve to have your efforts recognised. Why not make an occasion of the formal presentation of this money? Given sufficient notice, most banks are willing to supply 'large' cheques for the purpose.

Maybe your local paper might be interested in covering the presentation. Certainly your school will want a pictorial record of your achievement.

Your assignment is now almost complete. Write a brief letter of thanks to all those who have helped you in any way. This is not just an expected courtesy. It could also work to your advantage, should you ever look for their support in the future.

You may now breath a sigh of relief. You have finished this assignment.

Well Done!

Unit Five—Stereotyping

Female

Male

For this unit you should collect a wide selection of comics and magazines aimed at young people.

It is important also, that you should understand the following words:

Nurture	To encourage the growth and development of a child.
Equity	Fairness, justice.
Connotation	To imply something more than the obvious meaning.
Equality	The state of being equal.
Subservient	Respectful or slave-like.
Stereotype	An idea or an image that has become fixed or unchanged.

What is Stereotyping?

Stereotyping is an oversimplified and fixed mental image of a person which is shared or used or accepted by large numbers of people. It may be quite broad—Jews, white people, black people, women, men, or much narrower—members of a certain political party, feminists, estate agents. Stereotyping is normally accompanied by prejudice. Stereotyping people for whatever reason presents them as simple, less individual and more predictable than they are.

There are different types of stereotyping:

1. Sex-role stereotyping

2. Racial stereotyping

3. Occupations stereotyping

For the purpose of this unit, we will look at sex-role stereotyping because it affects everyone in the world. Your gender is still, probably, the most important factor in determining your experience of life. Unfortunately, however, this can pose many problems. Today, many of us believe that we are aware of the dangers of judging people according to their gender, but it is still surprising just how often we fall into the trap of stereotyping people by our use of **language**, our **attitudes** and our **expectations**.

Look at the list of opposite personal qualities below:

hard	brutal
emotional	quiet
assertive	soft
unemotional	tough
cold	strong
affectionate	gentle
brave	kind
timid	weak

Choose any ten qualities—in the case of each adjective chosen:

- put it in a sentence to describe a person—either male or female.

- swop your answers with a partner and read what has been written.

- discuss the results.

Did many of you choose qualities which have traditionally been seen as feminine to describe the women you wrote about? Likewise did many of you choose qualities which are traditionally seen as masculine in your description of men?

Look at this list:

MALE	FEMALE
tough	emotional
unemotional	weak
hard	affectionate
cold	timid
assertive	gentle
brutal	quiet
strong	kind
brave	soft

In the past these qualities were seen as either male or female and fully accepted as such.

- Would you admire a man who is brutal?

- Would you admire a woman who is timid?

- Is there any reason why a woman should not be assertive and strong?

Some people would argue that sex-role stereotyping begins at birth—or indeed, even before birth! If a pregnant woman comments that her baby is kicking a lot, it is not unusual for her to be told that 'it must be a boy' as it is generally believed that boys, even in the womb, are more active than girls.

It is still the case that once a child has been born the female child will often be dressed in pink and the male child in blue. One of the reasons why parents dress their children in either pink or blue could be to make it clear to outsiders whether the baby is a boy or girl. Should it matter?

'What are little girls made of?
Sugar and spice and all things nice
That's what little girls are made of.

'What are little boys made of?
Rats and snails and puppy dogs' tails
That's what little boys are made of.'

The choice of toys given to children is a further example of stereotyping. For the first year of life, babies are usually given cuddly, soft toys to play with. However, once they begin to play more actively, there is a glaring difference between the toys given to boys and the toys given to girls.

Playing teaches **skills** and **patterns of behaviour**. It is at this early stage that the foundation is laid for later attitudes and expectations.

Look at the list below:

toys	tea set
doll's pram	kite
boxing gloves	make-up set
train set	beads
Cindy doll	action man
toy soldiers	sword
marbles	gun
skipping rope	conkers
Meccano	model-making kit
building blocks	cowboy outfit

- Should boys and girls use the same toys?

- Would you buy a young boy a doll?

Think about this carefully and discuss the advantages that might result from giving such a present to a boy. Remember, in your discussion that playing teaches skills and patterns of behaviour.

If you have younger brothers or sisters think about the toys they have been given.

- How many of the boys you know have been given a pram or a tea-set?

- How many of the girls you know have been given a carpentry set or a set of toy soldiers?

- We know that children learn through play—so what is being taught by giving a girl a doll and pram or a tea-set?

- When a boy is given a carpentry set or a set of toy soldiers what message is being given to him?

In comics and books we can see very obvious examples of the stereotyping of characters. In many traditional fairy tales, the female is portrayed as helpless, vulnerable, foolish and pretty—e.g. Snow White, Sleeping Beauty, Little Red Riding Hood, Rapunzel etc., or else the females in these tales are shown as cruel, vindictive, vicious, jealous and ugly—e.g. the Ugly Sisters in *Cinderella*, the cruel step-mother in the *Children of Lir* or the wicked witch.

By contrast, most of the male characters in these stories tend to be brave, strong, heroic and of course, handsome. They invariably arrive in the nick of time to rescue the 'damsel in distress'.

You are, no doubt, familiar with the traditional fairy tales which you can see are giving a certain message so you will be interested to see how people have changed these stories recently to reflect their views on sex-role stereotyping.

Red Riding Hood

One afternoon a big wolf waited in a dark forest for a little girl to come along carrying a basket of food to her grandmother. Finally a little girl did come along and she was carrying a basket of food. 'Are you carrying that basket to your grandmother?' asked the wolf. The little girl says yes, she was. So the wolf asked her where her grandmother lived and the little girl told him and he disappeared into the wood.

When the little girl opened the door of her grandmother's house she saw that there was somebody in bed with a nightcap on. She had approached no nearer than twenty-five feet from the bed when she saw that it was not her grandmother but the wolf, for even in a nightcap a wolf does not look any more like your grandmother than the Metro-Goldwyn lion looks like Calvin Coolidge. So the little girl took an automatic out of her basket and shot the wolf dead.

Moral: It is not so easy to fool little girls nowadays as it used to be.

—James Thurber

There are a number of difficult and unfamiliar words in the following story—Ms Snow White wins Case in High Court. Use your dictionary to find out the meaning of the following words:

injunction	under duress
retribution	derelict
remorse	conjugal
travesty	ex tempore
tainted	inter alia

Ms Snow White wins Case in High Court

n a landmark decision handed down in Court yesterday by Ms Justice Goodbye, Snow White was granted an injunction against seven men. **Mark Miword** reports on the case.

Snow White was yesterday granted an injunction in the High Court in Dublin, restraining a total of seven men from entering on or interfering with the premises in the heart of the woods, which had been shared between them for ten years. The Court heard how Ms White had been abused for a total of ten years by the defendants, since she was seven years old. In an **ex tempore** judgment, Ms Justice Goodbye said that it was the worst case she had ever been forced to hear.

At the conclusion of the hearing, which lasted four days, there was uproar from the seven defendants, who had to be carried forcibly from the body of the Court. Gardai were forced to arrest three of the defendants as they emerged, and all pleaded guilty to a breach of the peace in a special sitting of the District Court, and were fined £2 each and bound over.

Yesterday was devoted entirely to the judgment, as evidence had been taken earlier from both the plaintiff and the defendants. In outlining the evidence which had been given, Justice Goodbye said that it was obvious that the defendants had, by their own admission, never made any attempt to offer retribution to Ms White, and that the worst aspect of the entire case was that they had shown no remorse for their actions over the years. In fact, the contrary was the case, as the defendants sought to justify their behaviour, and thereby compounded the wrong.

Justice Goodbye outlined the circumstances under which the case came before her. Ms White had been abandoned in the heart of the forest, when she was seven years old, by an agent acting on behalf of her stepmother, who wished to get rid of her. She pointed out, *inter alia*, that it was open to bring an action for cruelty on foot of this. Ms White, after wandering around for some considerable time, had then stumbled on a small house. Exhausted, she had lain down to sleep. Upon awakening, she was confronted by seven men, who were returning home from work as gold-diggers. Justice Goodbye made the point that Ms White was in no fit mental or physical condition, by virtue of her age and circumstances, to make any decision which could amount under any circumstances to mean 'the right to choose', in the legal sense of the word. Consequently, everything which took place following the initial encounter was tainted.

Messrs Dopey, Sneezy, Happy, Grumpy, Doc, Sleepy and Bashful proceeded to enter into a contract with Ms White, who was still exhausted, and in any event, of an age not legally held to be old enough to enter into a contract. Effectively under duress, Ms White agreed—following various promptings from the seven men—to look after the house while they were out gold-digging. She also agreed to cook and wash for all seven, to make all the beds, to sew and knit and generally look after their welfare. Ms Justice Goodbye said that the contract, apart from its earlier mentioned failings, was derelict further in so far as there was no limit to the contractual obligations entered upon by Ms White. In return for agreeing to those conditions, Ms White was allowed to sleep in the house, and also have enough food to eat. The contract was, in the words of Justice Goodbye, 'a travesty of natural justice'. She said also that Ms White must have been 'the handiest slave these seven men would ever have the good fortune to encounter'.

The seven men were so content with their lot that they took to singing songs upon their exit from the house each morning, and upon their return in the evening. Ms Justice Goodbye outlined the duties which Ms White was expected to perform. She was forced to get up two hours before any of the seven men, and prepare their breakfast. At the same time, she had to gather wood to light the fire and ensure that the house was clean by the time the seven decided it was time for them to get up. She herself did not get anything to eat until they left. On occasion, there was very little food left and she was forced to wait until dinner time before she ate properly.

With regard to the washing of their clothes, Ms Goodbye rehearsed the evidence that had been given to the effect that the seven never took any care of themselves when they were out digging for gold. Knowing that they had someone at home to do 'all the dirty work', their behaviour was such as to suggest that they were deliberately creating work for Snow White. Ms White had given evidence of the filthy nature of all seven men. They left their clothes where they fell before they went to bed, and she was expected to cater to their smallest whim. This, said Justice Goodbye, was somewhat at odds with the claim of the defendants' Counsel that all seven were self-styled New Age men in touch with their own feelings and emotions. Throughout all of this, the seven men continually reminded Snow White that on no account should she attempt to open the door during their absence. To this end, they warned her about all manner of dangers which she might face should she disobey them. Justice Goodbye pointed out that even though this 'warning' might well be grounded in a genuine concern for Ms White's 'welfare', the defendants had brought no evidence forward during the hearing to support their claim. The result of these 'warnings' was that Ms White lived in virtual isolation for many years, unaware that around the cottage a small township, Crumlin, had grown up.

As Ms White reached maturity, it appeared to her that the seven men became more 'friendly', in her own words, and she believed that they were viewing her in a different light from hitherto. Gradually, it became clear that some of the seven had designs on her. Justice Goodbye pointed out that it was left to Ms White herself to make clear that 'conjugal rights' had been no part of the original contract. The Justice took the view that this was 'outlandish behaviour' on the part of some of the seven, and that 'it was an extension of the contract which no right-thinking person would agree with'.

The defendants, said Ms Justice Goodbye, had given evidence to the effect that throughout their careers as gold-diggers, they had made what they described as 'a fair bit of money'. However, none of this wealth had ever found its way to Ms White, nor indeed had gone any way towards making her life in the house any easier. The Justice said that the only conclusion that could be drawn was that the seven had hidden their wealth, and that they had no intention, even at this late stage, of making any amends to Ms White. The Justice also pointed out that it was open to Ms White to enter a claim on the entire property in the woods, with a view to ensuring complete title to the entire estate. The Justice felt that 'any Court in the land would surely look most favourably on any such claim'. Consequently, Justice Goodbye said that she had no hesitation in making an order restraining all seven defendants from entering on or interfering with the house in the woods. Leave to appeal was refused.

After the disturbances, during which one of the defendants, Mr Grumpy, started to shout abuse at the Justice, Ms White appeared outside the Court with her close friend and supporter, Ms Rapunzel. Speaking to reporters, Ms White said that her life had been 'like a bad fairytale' for the past ten years.

Last night, a spokesperson for the Irish Council for Civil Liberties said that they wished Ms White 'all the best for the future' but that the judgment itself held 'grimm prospects' for other cases in that every person who thought they had a similar case as Ms White might now take an action, but that the action might fail, and thus 'hopes would be raised which might not be fulfilled'. The Council said that it was exploring the setting up of a Working Party to look at the implications of this case for all gold-diggers. At some time in the future they may, or may not, publish a report.

—from *Sweeping Beauties*
by Clodagh Corcoran

Exercise

- Explain in your own words Ms White's version of the story.

- Pick out *four* examples of humour in the report.

- What evidence is there to show that this is not a 'traditional' fairytale but is rather a story of our time. Pick out at least *four* examples.

Choose a traditional fairytale and rewrite it, avoiding all the obvious sex-role stereotyping traps. Do not replace one set of stereotypes with another. It is important to strike a balance. Think about the true capabilities of men and women. Your story should contain at least 200 words.

Although there are some comics which are geared to both girls and boys, these tend to be aimed at younger children, but despite this fact, we can still see examples of sex-role stereotyping.

Look at the following extract from *Dennis the Menace*. It is quite amusing, particularly Tommy's final triumphant comment.

Don't be afraid to laugh at examples of stereotyping. Once you are aware that stereotyping is present, you can be entertained by its very absurdity.

The following dialogue is taken from a cartoon strip. It shows Margaret, Tommy and Dennis, three schoolchildren, having an argument in the park. This is how it goes:

Dennis: The trouble with you, Margaret, is you think ya know *everything*.

Margaret: I know a lot of things *you* don't know!

Dennis: Well, I know something *you* don't know!

Margaret: What's that?

Dennis: I know you don't know as much as ya *think* ya know! Don't pay no attention to Margaret, Tommy, she's a *dumb-bell*!

Margaret: Well, you're an *addle-brained imbecile*!

Dennis: Oh, yeah? Well you're a bone-head!

Margaret: And you're a *dim-witted dolt*!

Dennis: What the heck's a dolt?

Margaret: If you *weren't* one, you'd *know*!

Dennis: You're a dopey *numskull*!

Margaret: You're a *brainless, idiotic incompetent*!

Dennis: Yeah? Well, you're a . . . a . . .

Margaret: You can't get the best of me, Dennis, I know too many words!

Dennis: Well, you're even worse than all them things you said *I was*!

Margaret: Oh? And what could possibly be worse than *those* things?

Dennis: You're a . . . a . . .

Margaret: I'm waiting. Go ahead, what am I?

Dennis: YOU'RE A . . . A . . . GIRL!!

Tommy: Boy! You sure told *her*!

Dennis: Yeah. With all her big words she can't top THAT!

from Dennis the Menace by Hart Ketcham

Some people will argue that examples like the extract from *Dennis the Menace* are harmless fun and that by looking for examples of stereotyping one is being a spoilsport or unnecessarily sensitive. However—whilst it is true to say that in isolation the extract is quite funny—is it possible that by constantly reading this type of material, a young person will eventually absorb and accept the messages?

Most comics, however, are targeted at either a female or male audience. Look at the titles of these comics which are aimed at readers in their early teens. Do they tell us anything about the comic? Look at the content of the comics. What messages are being given?

Choose your favourite story from a comic and write up next week's episode.

Remember that the cartoon which accompanies the dialogue in a comic is very important.

In the exercise below, the words spoken by the characters have been blanked out. Look at the cartoon. What do you think the storyline might be? Write your own story to suit the graphics.

Finally, you should look at magazines which target older teenagers, magazines such as *My Guy, Blue Jeans, Seventeen*. These generally tend to have stories with a romantic interest.

- These magazines are bought almost exclusively by girls. Why?

- Why is there no equivalent magazine for boys?

- Look at the messages in these magazines. What are you led to believe is the norm?

- From the titles of the magazines available for teenagers, it is easy to see for whom these publications are designed—e.g. *Princess, Jackie, My Guy*.

 Think up six titles for comics or magazines which are aimed at both boys and girls in their teens.

Experts Believe That . . .

- Girls do better academically in single-sex schools.

- Girls make more stereotyped subject choices and career choices in mixed schools than in single-sex schools.

- Boys demand and get more attention in mixed classes. On average they receive two-thirds of the teacher's attention in mixed classes. They are questioned more, encouraged more and praised more.

- Boys are more likely to be disruptive in class than girls therefore they get more attention from teachers in an attempt to distract and interest them.

Attention in Class

Sue-Anne Clennell, a teacher herself, wrote the following poem after reading in the newspaper that boys get more attention from their teachers than girls.

Boys Get More Attention From Their Teachers Than Girls

This is a subject I was not disputing
as I made John swallow the paper
he was pea-shooting.
The boys who have demanded
our attention since the womb
are now flicking rubber bands
across the room,
So I'm afraid Celia will have to wait
for my reply . . .
'Glen, get your finger out of
David's eye!'
'I would like to help you Jane if
I were able,'
(Just as soon as I get Ken from
underneath this table.)
Is it Gary, or myself, who is going
psychotic?
As he texras on the desk
something erotic.
'Is Craig away today with
unknown maladies?
' Oh, good, we can now study
Shakespeare's tragedies.
'No Carlos, we do not play
soccer in class,
'Yes, Janine, with any luck you'll
pass!'

—Sue-Anne Clennell

Discuss each of the 'Experts Believe That' statements.

- Do you believe that they are true?

- Ask your teacher whether her/his experience supports these statements.

- Look at the second statement on the previous page. Are you surprised by this?

- Give reasons why you think girls limit their choices in this way.

It is not just in the area of subject choice and behaviour that obvious differences can be detected. Look at the extract below taken from *The Irish Times*, 10 April 1992.

Men can do while girls just watch in text-book stereotypes

Irish education promotes sexist attitudes which can hold children back, say women observers. **Mary Cummins**, *Women's Affairs Correspondent, reports.*

Less than a quarter of all the people in primary school text-books are women. Boys are portrayed as brave and strong, girls as small and fearful. Adult men are fathers and have jobs. Adult women are either mothers or hold jobs—and the jobs they have are usually as teachers, nurses, shop-assistants or queens (the wives of kings rather than sovereigns). Women jobholders make up some 9.9 per cent of the women in text-books while 100 per cent of men have jobs outside the home.

This is still the situation in the vast majority of text-books for children in primary schools. 'Children are like sponges,' says Ms Joan Whelan. 'They pick up these signals.'

Ms Whelan, a Dublin primary school teacher, is a member of the Women's Studies Group and has worked with the Department of Education on eliminating sexism from school books.

Read the piece carefully. You will see that sex-role stereotyping is once again a predominant feature. Although many teachers would have believed that great changes had been made towards eliminating sexism in text-books, it is disappointing to learn that in 1993 the role models in these books are still blatantly stereotypical.

Look at the quotation below from Jean Jacques Rousseau—educationalist and philosopher in the early eighteenth century.

'The whole education of women ought to be relative to men. To please them, to be useful to them, to make themselves loved and honoured by them, to educate them when young, to care for them when grown, to counsel them, to console them and to make life sweet and agreeable to them—these are the duties of women at all times and what should be taught them from their infancy.'

You may think that these views are very extreme, but have things changed that much?

Nowadays, many women combine a career outside the home with their family responsibilities. In effect, a woman often has to combine two full-time jobs. In the past it was believed that caring for the family and the home was the woman's role. It was the man's job to provide. Fortunately, things seem to be changing and now many men play a far more active role in the rearing of their family and in household chores.

We are all very familiar with the term **housewife**, and although it is by no means the norm, there are some men who have chosen to become househusbands.

Sex-role stereotyping is still very evident in the career choices made by both boys and girls.

Number of female T.D.s in Dail Eireann	20
Number of male T.D.s in Dail Eireann	146
Number of female senators in the Seanad	4
Number of male senators in the Seanad	56

93% of those employed in agriculture, forestry and fishery are male. (E.E.A. Handbook, June 1989)

Teacher Training:

	FEMALE	MALE
Primary	1,493	339
Domestic Science	260	0
Physical Education	209	447

(*E.E.A. Handbook, June 1989*)

What do these statistics tell you?

Does the management structure in your school tell you anything about the place of women in education?

No unit on stereotyping could be complete without a brief look at language. Examine the list below. Using your dictionary check the meaning of the words:

vain	soft-hearted	macho	timid
boastful	virile	aggressive	promiscuous
boisterous	ambitious	compassionate	flighty
nervous	gossipy	scatty	businesslike
bullying	quiet		

- Which qualities are most often associated with males?

- Which are most often associated with females?

- Which could be used equally to describe both males and females?

 Look up the word **promiscuous** in your dictionary. Did you associate 'promiscuous' with male or female behaviour? Why?

Do you think that we adopt or use many double standards in our own use of language?

Why is it that when we use the term 'ruthless' to describe a man some people would see this as an admirable quality? However, the same word when applied to a woman is definitely not complimentary.

There are numerous other examples of double standards in language. Make your own list of words which you think have a possible double standard.

Consider how some people react to certain types of behaviour—are there any examples of double standards in the way they might respond? Think about how we might describe a girl who is deemed to be 'promiscuous'.

Promiscuous Behaviour

Male	Female
a bit of a lad	slut
boyo	whore
stud	easy
wild	hussy
macho	slag

 Look at the language used; the language used to describe the behaviour of the male tends to be almost affectionate—there is no element of condemnation.

Now look at the language used to describe a female who has behaved in *exactly* the same way. Each word is unpleasant, insulting and damning.

Language used in this way is said to be connotive. Remember at the beginning of this unit we explained that 'connotation' comes from the verb 'to connote' which means 'to imply something more than the obvious meaning'.

 If a certain mode of behaviour is judged to be unacceptable, then it is unacceptable for both sexes.

Would you agree/disagree with the above statement? Give *clear logical* reasons to support your answer.

There have been numerous studies carried out to prove that differences between males and females are the result of **nature** rather than **nurture**. In this context 'nature' means biological differences between male and female, whereas 'nurture' means upbringing, conditioning and education.

As we approach the twenty-first century, it is obviously in all our interests to try to live harmoniously. Yes, there are differences, but there is absolutely no reason why these differences should lead to discrimination.

You might enjoy reading the original version of 'Roger the Dodger'.

Unit Six—World of Work

You will find that there are huge differences between life as a student and life as a member of the work force. Once you enter the world of work you will have to take responsibility for yourself.

We are all aware that jobs are scarce and unemployment figures are high. The Jobless Total for September 1992 was 291,000 and it is expected to rise to over 300,000 during 1993.

In the past, when work was scarce here in Ireland, many Irish people emigrated to either Britain or the United States of America in search of work. Unfortunately, that route is no longer open to you as there is also an unemployment crisis in each of these countries.

You have all heard that the high unemployment figures are due to 'the recession'. How many of you know what the word actually means? The *Concise Oxford Dictionary* defines recession as—'a temporary decline in economic activity or prosperity'. You may wish to write this definition in your folder/notebook.

Although the signs are indeed gloomy don't be put off. There are jobs available. If you follow the correct procedures, you should be able to find a job.

So—read on!

Decision Making

Everyone has a secret dream to be someone special. You may want to become a professional footballer, boxer or model. However, in case your dream does not come true it would be very wise to make a few down-to-earth plans. Be realistic, recognise your skills and strengths, recognise also your limitations and weaknesses. Obviously if you have difficulty with Maths you should not look for a job in an accountant's office, but don't undervalue yourself. The secret of success is to look for a job in an area which suits you and for which you have a natural talent and in which you know you can succeed.

One of the ways of finding out where your talents lie is to complete an aptitude test. Remember **aptitude** means 'a natural talent for or ability'.

Aptitude tests try to measure your general ability, your verbal ability, your numerical ability. Your abstract reasoning power will also be assessed in these aptitude tests.

Which of the following types of job do you think would suit you? Which job do you think you would have an aptitude or talent for?

Place a tick ✔ in either the YES or NO box as appropriate.

	YES	NO
Working with shrubs and flowers in a nursery		
Working with dogs/horses		
Working on a farm		
Working on a building site		
Painter		
Carpenter		
Office work		
Receptionist		
Computer operator		
Store keeper		
Lorry driver		
Post-Office worker		
Shop assistant		
Hairdresser		
Child minder		
Serve in a restaurant		
Prepare food		

Now that you have a clearer idea of what work will suit you, the next thing you need to know is—where to look.

Looking for a Job

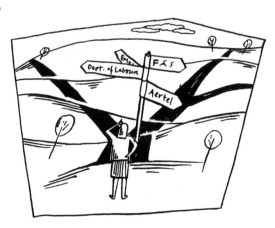

One of the first places you should visit is your local FAS Office. FAS has offices in most large towns in Ireland. You can obtain lists of the jobs and training schemes which are available in your area from these offices. FAS stands for *Foras Aiseanna Saothair*—Employment Training Agency.

The Department of Labour has a varied selection of career information leaflets which give details of the qualifications required for a large number of jobs.

There are various registered Employment Agencies, particularly in cities and large towns, which are always looking for suitable people to fill job vacancies.

Check the 'Situations Vacant' columns of the newspapers, especially local papers. Also check advertisements on supermarket notice-boards. You may have personal contacts who can tell you when a job vacancy occurs and who may also be able to arrange an interview for you with a prospective employer.

There are also **Job Spots** on radio.

Aertel is a television directory. Employers advertise their jobs on this directory. Those interested in a particular job may telephone for details.

Advertisement A

> **Wanted**
> **Sales Assistant for Fashion Boutique. Experience preferred but not essential. Written application only to:**
> **Ms Susan Murray**
> **Trendsetters**
> **29, Main Street**
> **Dunmanway**
> **Co. Cork**

Advertisement B

> **Wanted**
> **Sales Assistant for Fashion Boutique. Experience preferred**
> **but not essential. Apply for Official Application Form to:**
> **Ms Eavan Murphy**
> **Histyle**
> **Main Street**
> **Wexford**

Look at Advertisement A. Here you are required to write **a letter of application**. When a company puts a job advertisement in the paper, it often gets applications from hundreds of people. Only a few of these will be asked to come to an interview. So getting an interview is the big step. The purpose of your letter of application is to get you an interview. Of the many letters received, the neatest, clearest and shortest get read first.

Quite simply, longwinded, untidy letters don't stand a chance.

Look at the sample letter of application.

```
                                    26, North
                                    Street,
                                    Dunmanway,
                                    Co. Cork.
Trendsetters,                       22 August 1993
29, Main Street,
Dunmanway,
Co. Cork.

Dear Ms Murray,
   I should like to be considered for the position of
Sales Assistant in Trendsetters as advertised in the
Evening Echo on 20 August 1993.
   I am sixteen years old and I recently completed my
Junior Certificate at St Mary's Community School.
During the last year I worked on Saturdays at 'Anne's
Boutique', 76, Green Street, Dunmanway. The manageress
Ms Una Healy will be pleased to give you a reference.
   I am an active member of the Eastend Youth Club. I
am interested in fashion and design and I enjoy
swimming and tennis.
I would be delighted if you would consider me for the
position.
        Yours sincerely,

        Monica Bree
```

Write your own letter of application for one of the jobs below.

APPRENTICE MECHANIC WANTED

Apply giving details of age, educational qualifications, experience if any, to:

G. Murphy
STAR Garage
Tivoli
Cork City

**THE ROYAL HOTEL, ROSSLARE
CO. WEXFORD**

Require trainee Waiter/Waitress

To work in busy restaurant

Apply immediately to:

Ms A. O'Brien

Personnel Officer

**ENERGETIC AMBITIOUS YOUNG
PERSON REQUIRED BY BUSY
FLORIST**

Apply with all relevant details to:

Jane Moore
Daisychain
Main Street
Athlone

STORE PERSON WANTED

Hard working young person required by large supermarket. Apply giving all details to:

Manager
L & N Supermarket
Main Street
Wexford

You may use either the sample letter of application or the sample layout as a guide. In the letter you should:

- Refer to the advertisement
- State your qualifications/experience
- State your hobbies/interests
- Ask for an interview.

	Your Address
	Date

Advertiser's Name
Position
Company Name
Address

Refer to advertisement
State your qualifications/experience
Ask for an interview

Yours faithfully
Your signature

Before you fill in a job application form, you should take a photocopy of it first. Then you can do a rough draft.

Though application forms may have different layouts they all ask for the same basic information about yourself, e.g. name, address, date of birth, schools attended, subjects studied, grades obtained, interests/hobbies, referees.

ANY QUALITY FOODS LTD
Up St, Waterford

Tel: (05) 71797
(05) 71798
(05) 71799

Application for Employment

Fax: (05) 71799
Reg No.: XX35900
V.A.T. No.: XX35900

Date .... /.... /....

Name ....

Address ....

....

Telephone No. ....

....

....

POSITION APPLIED FOR ....

Age .... Date of birth .... / .... / .... Marital status ....

Health .... Do you smoke? ....

===

EDUCATION

Primary .... From .... To ....

Secondary .... From .... To ....

===

WORK EXPERIENCE

.... From .... To ....

.... From .... To ....

.... From .... To ....

.... From .... To ....

Do you hold a driving licence? .... Licensing Authority ....

Classes ....

Current employer .... Since ....

Reason for change .... Current wages ....

Notice required by present employer ....

Referees 1. .... 2. ....

....

....

Signed .... Date .... / .... / .....

You will see on the application form above that you are asked to give the names of two people who would be prepared to act as your referee, i.e. to give you a reference.

A referee in this case means—'A person who is willing to testify to character of applicant for employment'. Obviously your parents or best friend think you are a wonderful person, which may be why most employers expect that your reference should be written by either your school principal or a previous employer.

It is important that *before* giving a person's name as a referee, you should write to her/him asking whether s/he is prepared to write a reference for you. This shows that you are conscientious and courteous.

Task. Write to your school principal/previous employer seeking permission to use her/his name as a referee. It is important that you indicate the type of job for which you are applying.

Some employers may ask that you send on a **Curriculum Vitae*** with your letter of application or your application form. A C.V. is a very important document.

Look at the sample layout of a C.V. below. Using this as a guide write your own Curriculum Vitae.

***Curriculum Vitae** —means the course of your life.

First the title, be sure to spell **CURRICULUM VITAE** correctly as an error here is easy.

PERSONAL DETAILS

Name: full name
Address: full postal address
Telephone: including area code
Date of Birth: not your age
Marital Status:
Sex:
Nationality:

EDUCATIONAL RECORD

Primary: dates e.g. 1973-1981 name and address of school
Secondary: as above
Third Level: as above
Qualifications/Certificates
Intermediate/Junior Certificate
Subject: Irish
Level: Ordinary Grade B
Leaving Certificate
Subject: English
Level: Higher Grade C

EMPLOYMENT EXPERIENCE

Date:
Name/Address of Employer:
Position Held:

HOBBIES AND INTERESTS

This gives you the chance to tell the prospective employer about yourself. Use the more dynamic words like 'achieved' and 'attained' here instead of 'got'.
This section allows you to portray yourself as ambitious, competent, efficient, resourceful, versatile etc.

REFEREES

At least two are recommended. Get their permission first. Include their names, addresses and telephone numbers. Keep referees informed of your progress.

SIGNATURE AND DATE

The date on which you are applying.
Your C.V. should be typed, well laid-out and neat.

A polite follow-up by telephone, after a reasonable interval, is recommended.

Interview

Ask your Careers teacher or teacher of English to organise mock interviews for you. If you have access to a video camera, make a recording of the interview. Then watch the video tape.

Fill in the questionnaire below—what you learn about yourself may help you in a real job interview.

This Questionnaire is private and confidential.
Circle the answers that apply to you.

1. During the interview I was sitting . . .
   (a) Sprawled
   (b) Rigid
   (c) Fairly relaxed
2. During the interview my voice was . . .
   (a) Too loud
   (b) Clear and audible
   (c) Soft and mumbly
3. During the interview I established eye contact . . .
   (a) Not at all, I looked into space
   (b) I stared fixedly at the person to whom I was speaking
   (c) I looked at all the interviewers to include them in what I was saying
4. During the interview I used my hands . . .
   (a) To fiddle with a ring, lock of hair, etc.
   (b) To emphasise important points
   (c) Wildly and waved them about too much
5. During the interview when answering questions I . . .
   (a) Answered fully
   (b) Interrupted
   (c) Rambled off the point
   (d) Asked when I didn't understand
   (e) Repeated myself
   (f) Argued rudely when I disagreed with a point.

If you have not got access to a video camera, it would be worthwhile to tape-record your practice session. You will be surprised by the number of times you hesitated, stumbled and repeated yourself.

There are a number of obvious points you must remember on the day of your interview.

Appearance

It is very important to be clean, tidy and well-groomed.

In the past it was expected that male applicants would wear a suit, shirt, tie and appropriate shoes. Female applicants were expected to wear a suit or business dress and jacket and gloves! It is no longer necessary to dress so formally. However, it must be emphasised that you must not dress too casually. The employer must be able to see that you made a special effort—that you are taking this interview seriously.

Attitude

It is important, also, to have the right attitude. You are bound to feel nervous, but so is every other applicant. Don't let nervousness spoil your chances. An interview is a two-way process. You are two adults doing business—just as you are looking for a job, the employer is looking for someone to fill the vacancy. The employer is not offering any favours, s/he is looking for the best person for the job. Remember—you have no need to grovel—just present yourself positively.

Punctuality

It is vital to arrive on time for your interview. It will create a very bad impression if you arrive late. It will also cause you to feel anxious and flustered. Find out exactly where the interview is being held, and how to get there in plenty of time, particularly if you are travelling by public transport. Try to arrive at least ten minutes before the appointed time.

Remember to get some information about the company for whom you hope to work.

At the end of most interviews you are usually asked if you have any question which you would like to ask. It creates a good impression to do so. Prepare in advance a number of suitable questions.

There are a few further points to remember at the interview.

1. Knock on the door of the interview room before entering.

2. Sit comfortably, try to be relaxed but don't slouch.

3. Avoid one-word answers. It is not up to the employer to drag the information from you, so give full detailed answers.

4. If you don't understand a question don't be afraid to ask the interviewer what s/he means.

5. Don't be intimidated by pauses and silences. If you are satisfied with the answer you have given, don't elaborate further.

6. Be polite at all times and remember to thank the interviewers when the interview is over.

If, as you leave the room, you notice this . . .

. . . then it would mean that you had not followed the above advice.

Telephone Interview

Jobs advertised on Radio—**Job Spots**—or on Television—**Aertel**—sometimes ask that you telephone for further information. Obviously the employer can only judge you on what s/he hears so think carefully before you make the call.

Michael Ryan decided to ring 01–123456 to enquire about a vacancy in the music department of a large department store. Michael rang from a coin-box.

Read the following dialogue aloud with a partner:

Michael: Hi. Is that Clery's?

Receptionist: Yes, can I help you?

Michael: Yeah—this is Michael. I'm ringing about the job.

Receptionist: What job? To whom do you wish to speak?

Michael: I don't know really—I heard about the job on the local radio—well, actually, my mother heard it and she told me to ring this number about it.

Receptionist: We have advertised several positions recently. Do you know the extension number?

Michael: I did write it down, but I can't find it now. I must have lost it.

Receptionist: I'll connect you to our Personnel Department. Hold on please.

Personnel Officer: David Grey here. Can I help you?

Michael: Oh hello, I'm Michael.

Personnel Officer: Who?

Michael: Michael Ryan—I'm ringing about the job which was advertised on the radio—that's why I'm ringing.

Personnel Officer: Which position?

Michael: Oh the job in the Music Department. How much is the pay?

Personnel Officer: Well, firstly could you tell me about yourself—your age, what school you attended . . .

Michael: Oh yeah—but hold on—I must get more change—Oh I've only got . . . pip pip pip . . .

Michael made some very bad mistakes in his telephone conversation.

 Task: Write out in dialogue form the conversation as it should have happened if Michael had been better prepared.

The first few days in any new job can be very difficult. You'll feel awkward and ill at ease. You'll find that most people are helpful and understanding but it will take time before you feel confident. People hide their nervousness in different ways; some long to disappear into the paintwork, while others tend to become pushy and bossy. Do neither—just be yourself. Once the first few days are over, things will get much better.

For many workers one of the most important days is **Pay Day**.

Remember there is a big difference between **gross** pay and **net** pay. Your employer is legally obliged to give you a proper pay slip showing exactly what deductions have been made.

All workers who earn over a certain amount of money in a tax year will pay **Income Tax**. The income tax year is calculated from 5 April. If you are employed, you will pay tax under a system called PAYE.

PAYE = Pay As You Earn.

Each time you are paid, a certain amount is taken from your wages and paid to the Revenue Commissioners.

Here are some words from Helen O'Brien's pay slip. **Try to match the correct word with its meaning**.

Word	Meaning
employee	money paid towards a pension
overtime pay	money paid to the government
bonus	Pay Related Social Insurance (money paid for social insurance benefits and state pensions)
union subscription	money earned before deductions
net pay	money earned for working extra hours
superannuation	a person employed
gross pay	money paid to a trade union
PRSI	money paid for efficiency
income tax	take home pay

PAY ADVICE

Kalamazoo
business system   1807

Week or Month No.	Date	1 8/4/94	2 15/4/94	3 22/4/94	4 29/4/94		
✔ Insurable Employment		✔	✔	✔	✔		
EARNINGS Details		OT 6hrs					
A		120-00	120-00	120-00	120-00		
B	6 hrs OT	27-69					
C	Bonus	–					
D							
E							
Gross pay		147-69	120-00				
Pension/Superannuation	5%	6-00	6-00				
Gross Pay for Tax Purposes		141-69	114-00				
Gross Pay to Date for Tax Purposes		141-69	255-69				
Tax Free Allowance		65-00	130-00				
Cumulative Taxable Pay		76-69	125-69				
Cumulative Tax to Date		20-71	33-94				
Tax Refund							
DEDUCTIONS Tax	TABLE A	20-71	13-23				
P.R.S.I. Contribution	A1	10-98	8-84				
1 Union		2-50	2-50				
2							
3							
4							
5							
6							
Total Deductions		34-19	24-57				
Net Pay		107-50	89-43				
1 Travel Ex.		–					
2							
Total Amount Payable		107-50	89-43				
Employer P.R.S.I. Cont.		17-29	13-91				
Cumulative of Total P.R.S.I.		28-27	51-02				
Employee's Cumulative P.R.S.I.		10-98	19-82				
Your Pay is made up as shown above		Helen O'Brien	Helen O'Brien				

Look at Helen's pay slip carefully, then answer the following questions.

- What is Helen's gross pay?
- How much does Helen earn per hour?
- How much tax has Helen paid?
- What is Helen's union subscription?
- How much was deducted altogether from Helen's pay?
- What was Helen's net pay?

An employer can pay wages in three ways:

1. Cash

2. Cheque

3. Directly into a bank account.

Write down the advantages and disadvantages of each method of paying wages. Try to think of at least two advantages and two disadvantages of each method.

You will notice that Helen pays a union subscription. Why do you think she decided to join a trade union? Is there any need for a trade union movement?

The Trade Union Movement developed as a result of the Industrial Revolution which began in England in the eighteenth century. Many employers exploited their workers who had to work long hours in appalling conditions for very poor pay. Workers could also be dismissed at the whim of the employer.

To protect themselves workers joined together because they realised that there was strength in numbers. We can understand the importance of this solidarity through the old saying: 'United we stand, divided we fall.'

The *Concise Oxford Dictionary* defines 'solidarity' as: 'holding together, mutual dependence, community of interests, feelings and actions'.

Although things have improved enormously for workers and even though you will not now be transported to Australia for thinking about joining a union,* it is still very important that unions retain their strength.

A Trade Union should look after your interests—your earnings, the conditions in which you work, the hours which you work. If you have a specific work related problem, your union representative at work should help to solve it.

Remember, the strength of a Trade Union depends on its members. It is not enough merely to join a union and pay your union subscription/dues. You should participate actively in the affairs of your union by attending meetings, expressing your opinions and voting wisely. Trade Unions are usually referred to in the media by their initials.

I.N.O.	N.B.U.
I.B.O.A.	C.W.U.
A.S.T.I.	C.M.U.
S.I.P.T.U.	I.N.T.O.
T.U.I.	P.O.W.U.

Some of the initials above contain the word 'Union'. Some contain the word 'Association'. Some have the word 'Organisation'. Find out what the initials in the above box mean.

*Transportation to Australia for seven years was handed down to six Dorset farm workers (from Tolpuddle) who formed a lodge (union) to try to prevent their employers cutting their wages.

Like many others, you may find that your first job does not offer full job satisfaction, or it may not be sufficiently challenging. Don't despair—many choices are still open to you. You may decide to improve your qualifications by attending night classes or doing a correspondence course which would help you in your search for a new job. Whatever you decide to do, don't get into a rut.

The future is yours and you can decide how to shape it.

Unit Seven—Newspapers

By the time you have worked your way through this unit, you should have all the skills necessary to produce your own class newspaper. So, before beginning this unit we should perhaps explain the word 'Media'. Most of you are probably quite used to hearing the word but how many of you actually know what the word means?

Medium —*A channel through which information is transmitted: newspapers, radio, television. Media is the plural of medium.*

You might find it useful to copy this definition into your folder/notebook.

The *main* function of a newspaper is to give information to the reader. As well as presenting this information the newspaper also explains it.

A newspaper can act as a watchdog or public conscience by exposing public scandals. To do this however, the newspaper must have the freedom to report what it believes to be the truth. In some countries, newspapers are controlled by the government so readers are only allowed to read news articles which are approved by the government. The freedom to print what you believe to be true is known as the **freedom of the press**. This freedom is highly valued and is in part what differentiates a **democracy** from a **dictatorship**.

A newspaper can also entertain.

Traditionally, newspapers were privately owned. As you can imagine, a family which owned a newspaper had considerable power and influence.

Nowadays, however, the *Irish Press* is controlled by Irish Press News Ltd and Ingersoll Publications. The *Irish Independent, Evening Herald* and many local papers are controlled by the Independent Newspapers Group. *The Irish Times* is run by a trust and all the profits made are immediately ploughed back into the paper.

Types of Newspapers

Newspapers can be divided into three main types:

1. Quality newspapers
2. Tabloid newspapers } National newspapers
3. Local newspapers

Quality Newspaper. This is one which is accepted as having a very high standard of reporting. It does not report gossip nor does it use a sensationalist style of reporting. A quality newspaper deals in facts.

Tabloid Newspaper. Originally, the word 'tabloid' referred to the size of the newspaper. A tabloid was smaller than a broadsheet. (A broadsheet is the larger newspaper size on which papers like *The Irish Times* and the *Irish Independent* are printed.) Nowadays, however, the word 'tabloid' refers to a sensationalist style of journalism. The tabloids seem to be particularly interested in the private lives of stars and celebrities. Reporters working for tabloid newspapers have often been accused of being 'economical with the truth'. What do you think is meant by this expression?

Occasionally, some people refer to the tabloid papers as the 'gutter press'. Read the extract from Paul Dehn's poem below.

Gutter Press

News Editor
Peer Confesses,
Bishop Undresses,
Torso Wrapped in Rug,
Girl Guide Throttled,
Baronet Bottled,
J. P. Goes to Jug.

But yesterday's story's
Old and hoary,
Never mind who got hurt.
No use grieving,
Let's get weaving.
What's the latest dirt?

Diplomat Spotted.
Scout Garrotted,
Thigh Discovered in Bog,
Wrecks off Barmouth,
Sex in Yarmouth,
Woman in love with Dog,
Eminent Hostess shoots her Guests,
Harrogate Lovebird Builds Two Nests.

Cameraman: *Builds two nests?*
Shall I get a picture of
*   the lovebird singing?*
Shall I get a picture of her
*   pretty little eggs?*
Shall I get a picture of her babies?

News Editor: No!
Go and get a picture of her legs.

Beast Slays Beauty, Priest Flays Cutie,
Cupboard Shows Tell-Tale Stain.
Mate Drugs Purser.
Dean Hugs Bursar.
Mayor Binds Wife with Chain.
Elderly Monkey Marries for Money.
Jilted Junky Says
   'I want My Honey'.

Cameraman:
'I want my honey?'
Shall I get a picture
  of the pollen
   flying?
Shall I get a picture
  of the golden dust?
Shall I get a picture
  of a queen bee?
          —Paul Dehn

This poem is called 'Gutter Press'. Do you think that this is an appropriate title?

Give reasons why you think it is/is not.

Look at the structure of the poem. Each line in the first verse is a sensational newspaper headline. Now look at the second verse. Would you agree with the sentiments expressed there—'Never mind who got hurt'?

During the summer of 1992 a number of British tabloid papers published private photographs and articles about a member of the British royal family. These photographs and articles damaged this person's reputation and must have been very painful for her. We have already said how important it is that the press should have the freedom to print what it believes to be true but is there a danger that in allowing the press freedom we are denying the individual her/his freedom and privacy?

Organise a class discussion on this subject.

Local Newspaper. Local newspapers, as the name suggests, deal with local issues—political, economic and social. Local papers are usually published weekly. Generally, there are far more photographs in a local newspaper than in a national newspaper.

Do you think that having more photographs is likely to increase circulation? Why?

The circulation of a newspaper refers to the numbers of copies sold.

All newspapers have a number of features in common but there are distinct differences in what each type of newspaper offers.

Quality	Tabloid	Local
world news	national news	local news
national news	scandals	County Council meetings
politics	gossip	Corporation meetings
editorial comment	human interest	editorial comment
letters to the editor	sports	social events
business and finance	editorial comment	court cases
sport	horoscopes	cookery
arts and entertainment	puzzles	marriages, births, deaths
environmental issues	problem page	horoscopes
specialist interest	television/radio	advertising
marriages, births, deaths	advertising	
obituaries		
crosswords		
advertising		
television/radio		

Think carefully about the following questions. They will help you when you work on your own newspaper:

- Why does a quality newspaper not have a problem page?
- Why does a local newspaper carry reports of Council/Corporation meetings?

- Why does a local newspaper rarely deal with world news?

- Why would you expect to find quite detailed articles on business and finance in a quality newspaper?

- Why do you think that both quality and tabloid newspapers carry detailed sports sections?

- Do you think that the letters to the editor section serves any useful purpose?

Now that you know about the functions of newspapers and about the different kinds of newspapers it is time for you to think about your own class paper.

Your first decision must be about the kind of paper you want.

Is yours going to be a school-based paper? Are you going to cater to a wider market by attempting to write a locally-based paper? Perhaps you are going to be really ambitious and try to produce your own quality newspaper!

Before making your decision look again at the various features you would expect to find in each of the different kinds of papers. How easy will it be to collect the news and information you require? Organise a class discussion to make your decision.

Remember, there is no point in making life overly difficult for yourself or you will just lose heart and abandon the project entirely, so choose sensibly.

Your next exercise in this unit is to devise a suitable name and logo for your paper. The choice of name is very important as it can tell readers something about the paper.

Look carefully at the names of the newspapers below:

THE IRISH TIMES

Irish Independent

The Cork Examiner

What image do you think the owners are attempting to portray by using these names?

Do you think that anyone with a serious interest in the news would buy a paper called *The Daily Gossip*?

In the newspaper world the name given to the badge or logo and name of the newspaper is the **masthead**.

Before you go any further your next step must be to decide who does what. Obviously, it would be too difficult if all of you worked on each aspect of the paper, so choose what you would like to do. If you don't know the difference between a soccer ball and a rugby ball you won't make a very good sports writer, so make your decision, basing your choice on your interests/abilities. Obviously someone must be responsible for the decision about what information goes into a newspaper. The person who makes these decisions is called the **Editor**.

The diagram below shows the organisation and structure of a newspaper office. You may wish to use it as a guideline to decide who does which tasks.

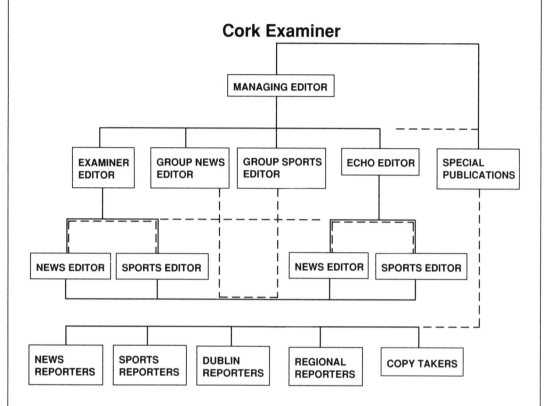

Your next task is to write to your local paper or to one of the national papers and ask whether one of their journalists would be willing to visit your class and talk to you about her/his work. Perhaps your editor could take on this responsibility.

A newspaper could not continue in existence if it did not make money for its owners. There are two ways in which a newspaper makes money:

1. Sales

2. Advertising.

Obviously the major source of income/revenue for any newspaper comes through its sales. So the aim of every editor must be to sell as many copies of the paper as possible. Generally, people remain faithful to their usual newspaper. Occasionally, however, a person will choose a different newspaper—an eye-catching headline might well be the reason for this. Therefore, the banner headline/front page headline is most important. Look at the following three statements. They are dull, dry and uninspiring. Try to think up witty, interesting eye-catching headlines for them.

1. Yesterday, Cork schoolboy John O'Shea got his head stuck in a toilet cistern.

2. Last Tuesday, residents of Tower Street were discussing plans to draw up a petition urging the closure of the nearby 'Cat's Eye' Nightclub.

3. A West of Ireland town was today discussing the news of the closure of a local factory which would lead to 400 redundancies.

You might wish to use puns in your headlines. A pun is a play on words which are similar in sound but quite different in meaning. The result is usually humorous:

- A matter of life and debt.

- Is life worth living? It depends on the liver.

Here are a number of headlines. Choose three and write the story that you think might go with them. The story may be as zany as you like; however, try to make it sound as if it might really have happened. Give as many factual details as possible—names, dates, places, reliable sources etc.

Hamster on mercy mission

Bouquet of barbed wire

Teenage mother bites Rottweiler

Hacksaw Harry's cutting edge

Smoking haggis causes alarm

Neighbours clean soap.

Now that you know all about headline writing, plan the front page headline and article for your own newspaper.

You should note that a newspaper article is written in columns and the space given to any story is measured in column inches. (1 Column inch = 25mm.) Set out your article appropriately.

You should also note that many articles can be distorted to reflect the writer's own viewpoint. This type of writing is called **subjective** writing.

A newspaper article which relates the facts and which is not influenced by the writer's own opinions is called **objective** writing. Most quality newspapers use what is referred to as standard English. This is accepted as clear and correct English. Slang would not be considered acceptable.

Using all this information now write your own front page article.

As we have said the other major source of income/revenue for any newspaper is through advertising. There are two types of newspaper advertisements:

1. Display advertising which usually advertises products.
2. Classified advertising which advertises jobs, items wanted or for sale.

The aim of a display advertisement is to sell a product. So, to attract the reader's attention the advertisement may be humorous, controversial or provocative. Although display ads may appear anywhere in the newspaper, classified ads always appear in the same place. Display ads tend to be much larger than classified ads.

Gather together examples of both types of advertisements. Then design your own ads to go in your class paper.

Perhaps someone in your group has a bicycle for sale or maybe someone else is looking for a stick insect.

Prepare your own display and classified ads. Remember that in classified advertisements you pay for the words used, so to save money you must be as brief as possible.

Obviously there is more to a newspaper than just the front page story and the ads so you should be gathering information for the inside features. Newspapers always carry features such as sports, television guide, deaths etc. on the same page every day. Why do you think that this is the case?

Editorials

The **Editorial** is often the means through which the views of the newspaper are expressed. The editorial also expresses the opinions of the owners or publishers on current affairs. Editorials are generally serious in tone and content.

Your next exercise is to collect a number of editorials from different papers. Try to find editorials which deal with the same subject and see if you can detect differing views and opinions. Do this exercise with a partner. Try to pick out any examples of **subjective** writing.

Think carefully about the power of an editorial in particular but also about the other articles in the paper.

- Do you think that it is possible for the owners/publishers to distort the news we read?

- Do you think that the press can be manipulated by owners/publishers or even by the large advertising companies?

- Do you think that it is possible for the owners/publishers to actually suppress certain items of news?

Using the questions above as a guide organise a class discussion on 'The Power of the Newspaper'.

To further attract the reader's attention, newspapers carry photographs and cartoons. These are visually stimulating and often memorable. The wording which goes with a photograph is called a **caption**. A caption either explains the picture or gives some background information to it.

Go through a few newspapers. Pick out a number of photographs which appeal to you. Cut off the captions. Mix up the photographs and the captions and present them to other groups in your class. Now check whether they can:

- Match the correct caption and photograph.

- Write an alternative but appropriate caption for each photograph.

Every newspaper will carry a number of articles other than the ones dealt with in this unit. Most newspapers will have articles on world and national news, sports, arts reviews and television guide. Write articles on these topics for your own newspaper.

Using the newspapers you have already collected look at the death notices and the obituaries. There is a difference between an obituary and a death notice. As the words suggest, a death notice informs us that a person has recently died. Most local newspapers and quality newspapers have a section carrying death notices.

An **obituary** is an article written about a person who has died. Usually that person is well known to the readers of the newspaper or has done something important for which s/he is remembered. Very often an obituary is written by a friend of the deceased and usually emphasises the positive/good aspects of the person's character.

Because most people accept the saying that 'one should not speak ill of the dead', you are unlikely to read the following in an obituary:

'*He was a bad-tempered old fool, loathed by all who knew him. His death didn't come soon enough.*'

Write obituaries for *two* of the following:

1. Breda O'Donnell, aged eighty-six. First female President of the Irish Engineers' Union.

2. Hacksaw Harry, singer with heavy metal band. Aged twenty-nine, died in motorbike accident.

3. Paul D. Vincent, aged seventy-two. Charity worker with many international relief agencies.

Most tabloid and local newspapers carry a horoscope section. Do you think that many people really believe what they read in their horoscopes? Are horoscopes just innocent fun or could they be harmful?

'It is the stars,

The stars above us,

govern our condition' —from *King Lear.*

Many people believe that the stars and planets influence our daily lives. Astrology is the art of judging these influences. In astrology, the year is divided into twelve star signs called the Zodiac. Earth, water, air and fire are the elements of the Zodiac. Find out which star sign belongs to which element. Look at the horoscopes given below:

ARIES (Mar 21–Apr 20)
Although financial pressures and plans are still very much on your mind, you can now afford to put a few possible developments off until later. You're so full of good ideas that all you need now is a little extra confidence.

CANCER (June 22–July 23)
This is a good time to keep yourself to yourself, to take the time and space to listen to your imagination and conscience. You may even consider cancelling a social engagement.

TAURUS (Apr 21–May 21)
It's time for a fresh start. Emotional and psychological spring-cleaning should encourage you to put the past behind you and face the future with an open heart. You seem to be keeping a secret, and may have to hang on for just a little longer.

LEO (July 24–Aug 23)
You may feel as if you are being forced to so something against your will or against your dignity. However, the best advice now is to press ahead and concentrate on making colleagues see your point of view.

GEMINI (May 22–June 21)
You may now have to come into the open, so have your story ready and make sure you're capable of making yourself understood. Throughout the day, you should find that your confidence recovers, and that it's no longer necessary to daydream.

VIRGO (Aug 24–Sept 23)
A splendid chance to travel to somewhere you have never been before is about to come your way. In any event, you will do yourself a very big favour if you develop all contacts with companions in distant parts and people from different cultures.

LIBRA (Sept 24–Oct 23)
Problems of a partnership or matrimonial nature should now be faced. You should find that once you talk about your concerns, they will begin to disappear and your confidence will return.

 CAPRICORN (Dec 23–Jan 20)
This looks like a busy day, and it is time to call on your more versatile talents. In view of emotional complications, it seems likely you will have to juggle several balls in the air at the same time.

 SCORPIO (Oct 24–Nov 22)
You still have no choice but to listen to other people, understand their feelings and try to satisfy their desires. Financial choices are now appearing, but there is no need for a final decision just yet.

 AQUARIUS (Jan 21–Feb 19)
The favourable planetary aspects you are now under are perfectly balanced by challenging ones, which means that this is an ideal moment to put your plans into practice. Thought and action should go hand-in-hand.

 SAGITTARIUS (Nov 23–Dec 22)
When dealing with finances, business or property matters you should make a point of being as clear-headed as you can. Your heart tells you one thing, your wallet another, so seek expert advice.

 PISCES (Feb 20–Mar 20)
If you are feeling at all isolated or confused it is because your planetary cycles are now changing and you are being obliged to stand on your own two feet, emotionally speaking. In future you will have to rely more on your own resources and less on support from outside.

Now devise your own horoscope for the zodiacal signs. Some people actually do believe their horoscopes, so remember they are horoscopes not horrorscopes!

As Francis Bacon said: 'Knowledge itself is power.'

Now that you know how a newspaper works, use this knowledge. Try to read a newspaper regularly. You will find that newspapers are not just a source of information but also a source of pleasure.

Unit Eight—Motoring

'Oh Lord, won't you buy me
A Mercedes Benz?
My friends all drive Porsches
I must make amends.'   —sung by Janis Joplin.

Unless you win the lottery, it is most unlikely that your first car is going to be either a Mercedes Benz or a Porsche, but, whatever car you do buy first, you must be looking forward to the freedom that owning a car will give you. Think about how owning a car will improve your image and you'll be amazed at just how popular you'll become! However, before you actually sit into your car, there are a number of important steps that you have to take.

First of all, think about the advantages of owning a car—no more hanging around waiting for buses. When the weather is bad you won't need to equip yourself with wellingtons, raincoat and umbrellas. Just think how easy it will be to get from one place to another—no waiting around for bus or train connections, no worrying about missing the last bus home. Finally, think about the safety aspect, particularly for females who are often very vulnerable waiting on their own at the bus stop, especially when it's dark.

Answer the questions on the Timetable below:

WEXFORD ENNISCORTHY GOREY EXPRESS

From Wexford

Wexford	08.10	10.30	13.05	17.20	21.45
Oylegate	08.15	10.35	14.00	17.25	21.50
Enniscorthy	08.25	10.45	14.10	17.35	22.00
Ferns	08.30	10.50	14.15	17.40	21.05
Gorey	08.45	11.05	14.30	17.55	22.20

From Gorey

Gorey	09.00	12.15	16.20	18.40	22.25
Ferns	09.15	12.30	16.35	18.55	22.40
Enniscorthy	09.20	12.35	16.40	19.00	22.45
Oylegate	09.30	12.45	16.50	19.10	22.55
Wexford	09.35	12.50	16.55	19.15	23.00

1. What time does the last bus leave Wexford for Gorey?

2. When does it arrive in Gorey?

3. How long does the journey take?

4. Eavan and Aengus Murray live in Oylegate. They go to college in Gorey. If college starts at 09.00 and finishes at 16.00:

    • At what time do they catch the bus in the morning?

    • At what time do they arrive in Gorey?

- How long does the journey take?

- At what time do they catch a bus home after college?

- When do they arrive in Oylegate?

5. There is a concert each Saturday evening in Oylegate. It begins at 19.30 and ends at 22.00.

- If people in Ferns want to go to the concert what bus will they have to catch?

- What bus will the people from Ferns have to take if they want to reach home that night?

- What do you notice about the time they will have to leave the concert?

You can see that for those people in Ferns who want to go to the concert and have to rely on public transport, there will be problems, so obviously there are advantages to owning your own car but are there any disadvantages? The most obvious disadvantage is, of course, the cost. You have to buy the car, pay for tax and insurance and then keep the car in good running order. Try to think about other disadvantages, not just to you but disadvantages on a wider scale. The points you might like to consider are pollution, congestion, land use, road deaths, etc. Divide into groups and organise a discussion or a debate on: 'The Environmental Hazards of the Motor Car'.

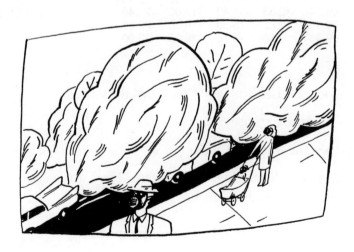

Remember that for a discussion or a debate to be successful, you must think carefully about the points you intend to make. An unprepared discussion can often just become a shouting match. With a partner, make a list of the points that you think are important. A debate must follow a formal procedure:

☛ *The speaker who is debating in favour of the topic (motion) is* **proposing** *the motion. The speaker who speaks against the motion is* **opposing** *the motion.*

☛ *At the beginning of your speech, you must address your audience. For example: 'Chairperson, Opposition, Classmates', etc.*

☛ *You must convince your audience through your* **arguments** *and* **research***, use of* **humour** *and your* **presentation***.*

Stage One

Most of you have probably decided, however, that there are more advantages than disadvantages in owning a car and so you are going to buy one. The first thing you must do is get a provisional licence. A provisional licence is a licence issued to allow a person to learn to drive and to apply for a driving test. You will be breaking the law if you don't have a provisional licence so *don't* begin your motoring career by committing an offence. Get a provisional licence by calling in or writing to your local government offices. The notes on the licence form are very detailed so read through them carefully.

APPLICATION FOR ISSUE OR RENEWAL OF   D.311.

PROVISIONAL LICENCE

(please complete this application in BLOCK letters and tick ✓ appropriate boxes)

DETAILS OF APPLICANT

1. Surname —————————————

2. First name(s) —————————————

3. Date of birth —————————————
    day   month   year

4. Country of birth —————————————

5. Permanent Address —————————————
    —————————————
    —————————————
    —————————————
    —————————————

6. Please sign your name on the upper part of this label.
   (This signature will be affixed to the licence.)

Signature —————————————

Name
and
Address

7. Please write your name and postal address on
   the lower part of this label in BLOCK LETTERS.

PROVISIONAL DRIVING LICENCE SOUGHT

8. Categories of vehicles for which provisional driving
   licence is sought.

	Vehicles				Vehicles and Trailer		
A	B	C	D	W	EB	EC	ED
□	□	□	□	□	□	□	□
A1	C1	D1				EC1	ED1
□	□	□				□	□

DISQUALIFICATIONS/ENDORSEMENTS

9. Is your driving licence or provisional licence at present required by court order to carry an endorsement?   Yes □   No □

10. Are you at present disqualified by a court from holding a driving licence or a provisional licence?   Yes □   No □

HEALTH AND FITNESS

11. Do you suffer from a physical disability which requires that adaptations be made to a vehicle to suit your disability?   Yes □   No. □

12. Have you suffered any deterioration in health which materially affects your ability to drive since you last applied for a driving licence or provisional licence?   Yes □   No □

13. Do you suffer from any of the disabilities or diseases listed on page 2?   Yes □   No □

14. Are you taking, on a regular basis, drugs or medicaments which would be likely to cause the driving of a vehicle by you to be a source of danger to the public?   Yes □   No □

15. Are you dependent on psycho-active drugs?   Yes □   No □

16. Have you ever suffered from alcoholism?   Yes □   No □

17. Have you ever suffered from epilepsy?   Yes □   No □

DECLARATION BY APPLICANT

18. I hereby apply to   Corporation/County Council for a driving licence.
I declare that the information given by me in this application is correct and that the accompanying photographs, certificates and other documents relate to me.

Signature of applicant   Date

This Declaration must be signed by the person to whom the licence is to be issued.

APPLICATION FOR ISSUE OR RENEWAL OF A

PROVISIONAL LICENCE

D. 311.

Please read the notes on pages 1 to 3 before completing the application form on page 4. The notes are a summary of the main requirements on applying for a provisional licence. They do not represent a complete statement of the law.

NOTES

A. PROVISIONAL LICENCE

A provisional licence is a licence issued to enable a person to learn to drive and to apply for a driving test. Driving with a provisional licence is subject to certain conditions in the interests of the safety of the driver and other road users. You must hold a licence for the category of vehicle you are driving (see page 3) and comply with the conditions attached to the licence while you are driving.

B. PERIOD OF LICENCE AND FEE

A provisional licence is issued for a period of two years and is subject to a fee of £12.

C. WHO MAY APPLY

You may apply for your first Provisional licence for vehicles in —

- category A1, B, C1 or W without any previous driving experience
- category A after you have held a full driving licence in respect of category A1 for at least two years
- category C, D1, or D after you have been granted a driving licence for category B or C1
- category EB, EC1, EC, ED1 or ED after you have been granted a driving licence for the appropriate drawing vehicle e.g. you must hold a driving licence for category C in order to apply for a provisional licence for category EC.

If you are an existing driver who already holds a provisional licence, or held a provisional licence or driving licence within the previous five years, in relation to a category of vehicles, you may apply to have a provisional licence issued or renewed in relation to that category of vehicles.

YOU MAY NOT apply for a provisional licence if you are disqualified by age, ill-health or otherwise. You may not apply for a third or subsequent provisional licence unless you underwent or applied for a driving test within the previous two years.
You may not apply for a provisional licence unless you are resident in Ireland.

D. PHOTOGRAPHS

Your application must be accompanied by two passport-type photographs. The requirements are:—

- two identical photographs (colour or black and white) size approximately 3.5 x 4.5cm
- reverse side of both photographs to be signed by you
- show full face without headgear against a neutral colour background
- reverse of both photographs to be neutral colour and unglazed

Approximate size of photographs needed

E. BIRTH CERTIFICATE

Your application must be accompanied by a birth certificate unless —

- you hold a current driving licence or provisional licence, or
- you held a driving licence or provisional licence within the last five years, or
- you hold a current valid driving licence issued by another Member State of the European Communities or another "recognised country".

F. CURRENT/LAST LICENCE TO ACCOMPANY APPLICATION

Your application for the issue or renewal of a provisional licence must be accompanied by:—

- your current or most recently issued driving licence, if you hold a driving licence or held one within the previous five years, and
- your current or most recently issued provisional licence if you hold a current provisional licence or held one within the previous five years (unless your most recent provisional licence has been superceded by the issue of a driving licence).

G. EYESIGHT REPORT

An application for a provisional licence for category A1, A, B, EB or W must be accompanied by a satisfactory eyesight report (ref. D. 509) unless —

- you have previously submitted an eyesight report with an application for a provisional licence, or
- your application is accompanied by a satisfactory medical report (see note H), or
- you have previously submitted a satisfactory medical report which is still applicable.

If an eyesight report is required in your case you should

- obtain a copy of an eyesight report form (ref. D. 509)
- have your eyesight tested by a registered opthalmic optician or by a registered medical practitioner
- ask him/her to complete the eyesight report.

You must sign the Declaration on the eyesight report in the presence of the optician or doctor.

It is now compulsory to have an eye test before applying for your provisional licence so make an appointment with your doctor or optician.

The reasons for the eye test are obvious, particularly if you are familiar with the cartoon character Mr Magoo. At the moment, it is not necessary to have a hearing test before applying for a licence. Do you think it would be a good idea to have such a test? List reasons in favour of such a test.

Now that you have had your eye test, got a copy of your birth certificate and signed photographs, you can fill in your application form and send it to your local County Council office.

1. At what age can you apply for a Licence to drive each of the following vehicles:

- Minibus

- Truck

- Car

- Motorcycle

- Tractor

2. What type of vehicles are included in Category E.C.1?

3. What is meant by 'passenger accommodation'?

4. What is meant by 'Design g.v.w.'?

CATEGORIES OF VEHICLES/MINIMUM AGE OF DRIVER

Vehicles are divided into categories and sub-categories for driver licensing purposes. You must hold a licence in relation to the type of vehicle you are driving. The Table below describes broadly the categories and sub-categories of vehicles and the necessary minimum age of a licensee. The Table is followed by a more detailed description of the categories and sub-categories.

Table

CATEGORIES OF VEHICLES

DESCRIPTION OF VEHICLE	CATEGORY		MINIMUM AGE OF LICENSEE
	Without Trailer	With Trailer	
MOTORCYCLES	A	—	18
CARS	B	EB	17
TRUCKS	C	EC	18
BUSES	D	ED	21
Motorcycles not over 125 c.c.	A1	—	16
Trucks not over 7,500 kg design g.v.w.	C1	EC1	18
Minibuses	D1	ED1	21
WORK VEHICLES/TRACTORS	W	W	16

DETAILED DESCRIPTION OF CATEGORIES OF VEHICLES

CATEGORY	VEHICLE
A1	Motorcycles not over 125 c.c., with or without sidecar
A	Motorcycles with or without sidecar
B	Vehicles with passenger accommodation for 8 persons or less and with a design g.v.w. not over 3,500 kg
C1	Vehicles with passenger accommodation for 8 persons or less and with a design g.v.w. over 3,500 kg but not over 7,500 kg
C	Vehicles with passenger accommodation for 8 persons or less and with a design g.v.w. over 3,500 kg
D1	Vehicles with passenger accommodation for more than 8 persons but not more than 16 persons
D	Vehicles with passenger accommodation for more than 8 persons
EB	Vehicles in category B with a trailer attached
EC1	Vehicles in category C1 with a trailer attached
EC	Vehicles in category C with a trailer attached
ED1	Vehicles in category D1 with a trailer attached
ED	Vehicles in category D with a trailer attached
W	Work vehicles and land tractors, with or without a trailer attached.

"Passenger accommodation" means seating accommodation for passengers in addition to the driver.
"Design g.v.w." means design gross vehicle weight (i.e. design laden weight). Manufacturers generally refer to it as gross vehicle weight (g.v.w.) and it is usually displayed on a metal plate attached to the vehicle by the manufacturer.

RF. 1A

Tax Renewal Form

R ☐

WARNING: THIS FORM MAY BE USED ONLY

If there is **no change of Registration Particulars, i.e., ownership, use, class, engine,** etc., since the last declaration.

Otherwise the appropriate Declaration Form must be completed. (See Note 2 overleaf)

ALL QUESTIONS MUST BE ANSWERED   (11/87)

This Application must be accompanied by:—

(a) A Remittance
(b) The Registration Book
(c) A current Certificate of Insurance under Road Traffic Acts 1961/68

Tick appropriate Boxes thus: ☑

APPLICATION

I apply for a Licence (Tax Disc) for the vehicle described below for the period set out at 2 below.

FOR OFFICE USE ONLY		
Licence Serial Letter		Reg. Book No.
12		
13	Gap Code	
	Renewal CHG ADD	Assessment
14	1 2	Arrears 15/4
15		Prev Exp
19		Arr Begin New Licence No
23		New Lic Begin
27		Amt
33		recd
39		issd
45		Checked
48		

1 REGISTRATION NUMBER ➞

2 Last Licence (Disc) expired		Month	Year	
	on the last day of			
Arrears Period (if applicable)	from the first day of			£
	to the last day of			
New Licence (Disc) Period	from the first day of			£
	to the last day of			

☐ Cheque   ☐ Money Order
☐ Cash   ☐ Postal Order

Place ✓ in appropriate box

TOTAL £

3 MAKE: MODEL:

4 CHASSIS NUMBER: ➞

BATCH NO.

5 INSURANCE PARTICULARS

Name of Insurance Company

....

....

Date of Expiry of Certificate under Road Traffic Acts 1961/68

53		
Day	Mth	Year

7 STATE COLOUR(S)

....

and tick nearest basic colour(s) below.

	61			
Black	A	Yellow	G	
Grey	B	Green	H	
White	C	Blue	J	
Beige	D	Purple	K	
Brown	E	Pink	L	
Orange	F	Red	M	
	Multicoloured (if more than two)		N	

6

Taxation Class ....
(e.g. Private, Goods, Cycle, Agricultural Tractors, etc.,)

8 DECLARATION   (See Note 5 overleaf)

I DECLARE THAT

(i) The particulars above are correct

(ii) The vehicle is normally kept by me at

....

(iii) The vehicle has not been used by me or with my consent in a public place (since the date of expiration of last licence.) (See Notes 5(b) and 6(a) overleaf)

} Delete if inappropriate

IMPORTANT
⬆⬆

9 Name and Address of Applicant in Block Capitals
(Public Limited Companies and Private Firms see Note 5 overleaf).

SURNAME or Company Name 63		*
Title (e.g., Mr., Mrs., Miss, Rev., Dr., etc.)		*
First Name(s)		*
Address		*
		*
		*
		*

NB ➡

APPLICANT'S SIGNATURE _____

Date ....

Signature of Garda ....

Date ....

Garda Station Stamp

RECYCLED PAPER

Look at the Tax Renewal Form above.

Find what is meant by:

- Remittance

- A *Current* Certificate

- Registration

- Expiry

- Delete if inappropriate

Stage Two—Learning To Drive!

From bitter and painful experience, most people will advise you not to ask your mother/father or girlfriend to teach you to drive. It can lead to frayed tempers, rows, tears and the learner/driver storming off in one direction vowing never to learn to drive nor even to get into a car again and the teacher/driver cursing her pupil's stupidity and vowing never to let her/him behind the wheel again. For the sake of your sanity and to learn properly, go for lessons to an approved driving school. Lessons are expensive but you will have a trained teacher and you'll be properly insured. Look in your *Golden Pages*. Check whether any of the driving schools in your area have any special offers.

There is a driving school in London called 'The Impact School of Motoring'. Do you think this is an appropriate name?

Think about what you are looking for from your driving school, then design a brochure for a school. Remember the name is important.

Now that you have booked your first lesson you suddenly feel that the world is your oyster. You have an image of yourself cruising along the highway in an open-topped sports car, your hair blowing in the wind and the companion of your choice sitting impressed beside you. Dream on, briefly, then come back down to earth: you have a long way to go before you reach that stage.

Not only do you have to learn how to drive, you also have to learn the rules of the road. When you got your provisional driving licence form, you probably also got a copy of *Rules of the Road*, published and distributed on behalf of the Minister for the Environment. Learn the rules carefully because, when you take your driving test, you will be tested on your knowledge of the rules of the road. You will fail your test if you are unable to answer the questions even though your driving may have been careful and correct.

Some of the language in the booklet is quite difficult and some of the sentences are very long-winded.

Look at the section on 'Roundabouts' from *Rules of the Road*, and rewrite the rules in simple clear English.

Remember that there are many people who have difficulty with reading so rewrite the rules with them in mind.

ROUNDABOUTS

The provisions of the Road Traffic Acts and the Road Traffic (General) Bye-Laws 1964 apply to traffic on roundabouts in exactly the same way as to all roads. In summary these require motorists to drive in a manner which takes account of the prevailing conditions, at a safe speed and having regard to lane discipline. The specific rule relating to roundabouts contained in Bye-Law 21 of the Road Traffic (General) Bye-Laws, 1964 requires that **"a driver shall enter a roundabout by turning to the left"**.

The following should also be noted carefully:

You should:

• Treat the roundabout as a normal junction which means you yield right of way to traffic already on the roundabout.

• **IF LEAVING BY THE FIRST EXIT** approach and enter the roundabout in the left-hand lane signalling a left turn and proceed to leave the roundabout at that exit.

• **IF LEAVING BY THE SECOND EXIT** approach and enter the roundabout in the left-hand lane but do not signal until you have passed the first exit, then signal a left turn and leave at the next exit.

• **IF LEAVING BY ANY SUBSEQUENT EXIT** approach and enter the roundabout in the right hand lane signalling a right turn. Keep in the right hand lane (i.e. the lane next to the centre). As you pass the exit before the one you intend to leave by, signal a left turn and, when your way is clear, move to the other lane and leave at the desired exit.

Remember that signals are merely indications of intent. They do not confer right of way. **When in doubt, play safe - YIELD.**

MAKING A LEFT TURN	TRAVELLING STRAIGHT AHEAD	MAKING A RIGHT TURN
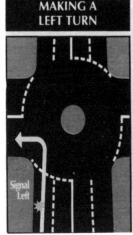		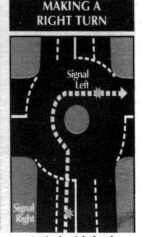
Stay in the left hand lane, indicate 'left' as you approach and continue to indicate until you have passed through the roundabout.	Stay in the left hand lane, but do not indicate 'left' until you have passed the first exit. Where conditions dictate otherwise, you may follow the course shown by the broken line.	Staying in the right hand lane, indicate right on your approach and maintain this signal until you have passed the exit before the one you intend to take. Then change to the 'left' turn indicator.

Look at the list of warning and/or regulatory signs below. Working with a partner and without using the *Rules of the Road* handbook, see if you can work out what the signs mean. Write down your answers.

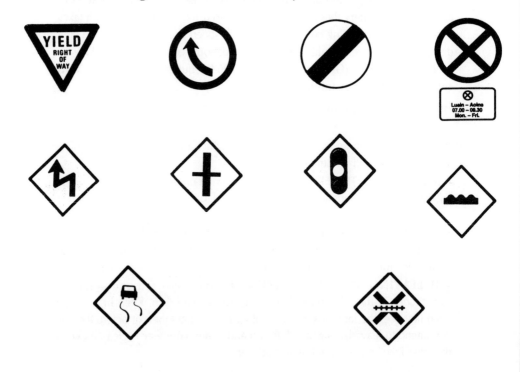

Now check your answers on pages 65–68 of *Rules of the Road*.

Stage Three—Buying A Car

Most people would prefer to buy a new car but that's probably out of the question for you so you'll have to settle for a second-hand car. What type of car do you want? Look in your local newspaper and visit your local car dealer to get an idea of the choices available and of the prices being asked. When you start to look at car advertisements, you seem to enter a whole new world, the language is often very technical and the terms used are difficult to understand.

Explain the following words, phrases and abbreviations:

Rear Spoilers	Catalytic Converter	G.T.	999 cc Fire Engine
4-Wheel Drive	Mint Condition	P.M.O.	Man/Auto
5 Dr	5 Sp	A.B.S.	P.A.S.
Power Steering	50 k	R.H.D.	S.R.

Analyse this advertisement taken from the *Wexford People*. Is there an element of dishonesty about it? As a group, discuss the advertisement.

Although cars are usually referred to as 'she', many of the images used in car advertising are definitely male. Think about the words used to describe the performance of cars. Also think about the shape of the sportier type car. Recently, however, car advertisers have adopted a gentler, more caring note in their advertising techniques. Why do you think this is? Perhaps the phrase 'the green Nineties' will give you some idea. Whatever kind of advertising is used by companies, advertisements play a large part in selling cars.

List the needs and requirements of the following people and, using that information, plan an advertising campaign for a **new range** of **cars** aimed at the following target groups:

- A general practitioner (GP) with a large and widespread rural practice.

- A young couple with three small children.

- Your teacher.

- A farmer.

- A young company executive.

Remember, the choice of car name should be apt and appropriate. Match the brand names of the cars below with the manufacturer.

Manufacturer	Brand Name
Ford	Primera
Toyota	Pony
Renault	Delta
Opel	Civic
Mitsubishi	Riva
Fiat	Ibiza
Volkswagen	Justy
Nissan	Kadett
Honda	Galant
Hyundai	Orion
Lada	Corolla
Seat	Uno
Subaru	Clio

Stage Four—Insurance

A person can make provision against possible loss, damage, injury or sickness by paying an agreed sum either weekly, monthly or yearly to an insurance company. This agreed sum of money is called the **premium**.

You are obliged by law to have motor insurance when you drive. If you are not correctly insured, you are not only breaking the law, but you are being very foolish, because if you have an accident without being insured, you will have to pay the full cost of repairs, yourself. If you injure someone else, you will have to pay all their medical costs and possibly compensation as well. So, be sensible, be insured!

There are three types of motor insurance:

1. Third party
2. Third party fire and theft
3. Comprehensive.

Insurance policies are often very difficult to understand and you will probably come across a number of new words and phrases.

Policy	Contract of insurance.
Indemnity	Protection, security, compensation.
Premium	Sum of money paid to the insurance company.

Third Party Policy. In the case of an accident, this policy protects the insured person against claims by other people or damage caused by the insured person to other vehicles.

Comprehensive Policy. In the case of an accident, this policy protects the insured person against claims by other people or damage caused by the insured person to other vehicles. It also compensates the insured against claims for damage to her/his own vehicle.

Agent. A person who has authority to sell policies on behalf of an insurance company.

You are now ready to begin your driving career so good luck but one final note.

Don't drink alcohol and then drive your car.

Throughout the year, and particularly at Christmas-time, there is a campaign to alert drivers to the dangers of drinking and driving. There is an increased garda presence on the roads as a warning to motorists that they may be stopped and breathalysed.

Your final task in this unit is to plan your own anti-drink driving publicity campaign. Look at television advertisements to see just how much information can be packed into 30– 60 seconds. Look at the tricks advertisers use—jingles, catchy tunes, well-known people, etc.

Working with a partner, plan a publicity layout. You might like to use a **story board technique**. Don't panic if you are not familiar with the term 'story board technique'. It means exactly what it says. It is a procedure used by people making advertisements or planning an episode of a soap opera. All it means is that you plan out your advertisement/campaign/episode using both words and pictures.

Using pictures obviously has visual impact. If you want to show what a character is thinking you can have a close-up of her/his face and expression and then her/his thoughts can be written into a speech bubble. It is really very simple. Remember that you want to attract people's attention, you want to shock them but, to shock, you don't need lots of blood and guts. Work on this campaign carefully. Who knows, if it is powerful enough, it could be adopted locally for next year's Christmas campaign. It could save lives.

Safe and Happy Motoring!

'I've been driving in my car
It's not quite a Jaguar!'—Madness

It's not quite a Jaguar—it's a banger. Sadly, for Sean Murphy, things haven't gone as well as he would have wished.

Read 'The Breakdown'. Do all the tasks.

MAP OF BREAKDOWN AREA

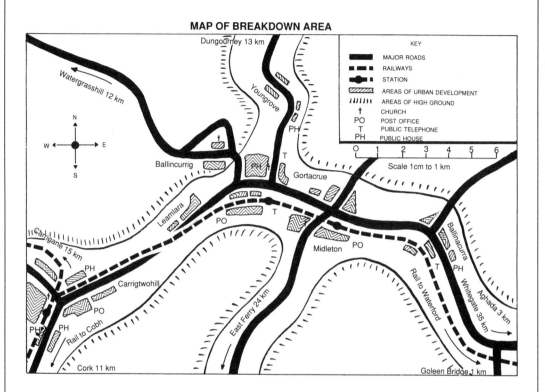

The Breakdown

Sean Murphy was from Dublin. He and his parents were spending Christmas in the country. It was a break, they said, a chance to escape the hustle and bustle of the city.

Sean had driven into Midleton quite early that Saturday morning to take his brother Michael to the station. Michael was returning early to Dublin. Sean was longing to be back at home in front of a blazing fire with a cup of tea. The road was treacherous as it had been snowing all morning. It was the main road from Dungourney to Whitegate. Sean and his parents were staying at 63, Viking Place, Dungourney. Sean had borrowed his father's car for the trip to Midleton. The car, or more accurately 'the Banger', was an old Renault 4L. There were 93,000 miles on the clock. It had definitely seen better days, but his father had the knack of fixing it whenever it broke down.

Sean drove slowly and carefully. He still had quite a long way to go to reach Dungourney. He wasn't a very experienced driver and the dangerous weather conditions made him extra cautious. He said a silent prayer as he passed the church at Gortacrue. He drove up a fairly steep hill. The engine began to rattle . . . 'Oh, I don't believe it, not now' Sean muttered aloud as he urged and cursed the car to the top of the hill until he reached a narrow village street. He'd just passed the local pub when the car spluttered and ground to a halt. He tried the ignition, but the engine just turned over and went dead. It was obvious that he wasn't going to get it moving without help from a garage.

Sean got out and slammed the door angrily. He felt like kicking the car. He looked around. He wasn't sure exactly where he was but he knew it couldn't be far to Youngrove. He then remembered that his father always kept a few maps in the glove compartment. Sean poked his head back into the car and pulled out a bundle of papers. There was a map and a copy of the A.A. Handbook—what a pity his father wasn't a member, he thought. Still, the map would show him exactly where he was, and the A.A. Handbook gave a list of garages in the area. He hoped to be able to get help without too much trouble.

AA Handbook (extract)

Garage facilities available in the area of the breakdown

Leamlara	APP		Tedcastles (Tel. 631111)
Gortacrue	APP	🚚	Savage's Filling Station (Tel. 632567)
	APP		Gortacrue Motors (Tel. 613224)
Midleton	APP	🚚	Motor Link Ltd., Cork Road (Tel. 613443)
	APP	🚚	Richard O'Connor, Riverside Way (Tel. 632492)
Ballinacurra	APP		Moloney's Garage, (Tel. 632789)
Carrigtwohill	APP	🚚	Roche's Garage, (Tel. 883112)

APP	Appointed garage
🚚	Breakdown appointment

Put yourself in Sean Murphy's position. Can you carry out the following tasks to get the car to a garage to be fixed and to get yourself home?

The car registration is **XZX 517**.

Tasks:

- Look at the map of the area. Work out where your car is on the map and mark the estimated position on it. Using the key of symbols provided and noting the scale of the map, estimate how far it is to the nearest 'phone box and write it onto the map stating which direction you will have to walk.
  (North, South, East, West)

- Using the A.A. Handbook, list a number of possible garages, and then decide on the nearest garage which can provide a breakdown and major repair service. Write down the telephone number in your folder and explain your choice of garage.

- You must now make a 'phone call to the garage you have chosen. When you telephone, you find that the garage office is closed for lunch but you are able to leave a tape-recorded message. Using the school tape-recorder, dictate the message, giving all the details which the garage will need to find your car.

- You have walked back to your car. The local pub has opened and you decide to have a snack while you wait for the breakdown service to arrive. They arrive just after 12 o'clock and tell you that the car will have to be towed away. You decide not to wait around but to use your time to do some Christmas shopping in Waterford.

Bus Timetable

Service 109   AGHADA – WATERFORD

Aghada (Bus Station)	07.00	07.30	22.00
Castlemartyr (High Street)	07.20	07.50 and every	22.20
		30 minutes	
		until	
Killenagh (Market Square)	07.40	08.10	22.40
Waterford (Bus Station)	07.55	08.25	22.55

Notes

* The following buses stop at Castlemartyr for 15 minutes, arriving at Aghada 15 minutes later than schedules.

Depart Aghada 08.00, 09.00, 10.00, 14.00, 15.00, 16.00, 17.00.

* **The following buses do not run on Saturday and Sunday**

Depart Waterford 07.00, 13.00, 17.00, 19.00

BUS EIREANN

BUS EIREANN

Schedules &
Time Tables

FOR INFORMATION PHONE

BUS EIREANN
Capwell Garage Cork ....(021) 508188

– to get you out and about

THE ONLY WAY TO TRAVEL

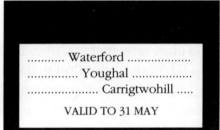

.... Waterford ....
.... Youghal ....
.... Carrigtwohill .....

VALID TO 31 MAY

CARRIGTWOHILL   MIDLETON   AGHADA   DUNGARVAN

GORTACRUE   GOLEEN BRIDGE   YOUGHAL   WATERFORD

See separate leaflet for details of fares

Season Tickets, Tickets in advance, Reservations

By personal or postal application to your local station, or your Travel Agent (not Season Tickets).

For specific information about weekday, train services use the 'Talking Timetable'	
Waterford	Tel: 949885
Midleton	613224
Cork	884678
Gortacrue	624566

Train service information

Write or phone Information Office at:

Station	Tel.	Open	
Waterford	949857	Weekdays	07.00–21.00
		Sundays	00.00–23.00
Dungarvan	948378	Weekdays	06.15–10.40
Youghal	898475	Weekdays	07.30–21.00
Exchange		Sundays	09.00–21.00
Aghada Point	769543	Weekdays	06.30–20.50
		Sundays	00.30–22.30
Goleen Bridge	54510	Weekdays	00.45–22.30
		Sundays	09.00–14.00
			15.30–22.15
Midleton	613266	Weekdays	06.55–22.30
		Sundays	09.00–14.15
			15.30–22.15
Gortacrue	624567	Weekdays	07.00–22.30
		Sundays	09.00–14.16
			15.30–22.16
Carrigtwohill	884993	Weekdays	07.10–22.30
		Sundays	00.30–12.00
			13.50–22.00

The bus service does not go into Youngrove but you can get the train from Gortacrue which will take you directly to Waterford. As an alternative you may take the train from Gortacrue to Aghada and you should be able to get the bus from there to Waterford. The publican has both a rail and a bus timetable on display in his premises. He says it will take you about an hour to walk to Gortacrue Station. By now it is one o'clock and you decide to leave right away.

TRAIN TIMETABLE

Mondays to Saturdays

WATERFORD P	d.	11.10	12.10	12.30	13.10	14.10	15.10	18.10	16.36
DUNGARVAN FP	d.	11.22	12.22	12.42	13.22	14.22	15.22	16.22	16.48
YOUGHAL P	a.	11.32	12.32	12.51	13.32	14.32	15.32	16.32	16.58
YOUGHAL P	d.	11.34	12.34	12.55	13.34	14.34	15.34	16.34	17.02
AGHADA FP	d.	11.47	12.47	13.08	13.47	14.47	15.47	16.47	17.15
GOLEEN BRIDGE FP	d.	11.54	12.54	13.15	13.54	14.54	15.54	16.54	17.21
MIDLETON FP	d.	11.59	12.59		13.59	14.59	15.59	16.59	17.26
GORTACRUE FP	d.	12.02	13.02	13.22	14.02	15.02	16.02	17.02	17.29
CARRIGTWOHILL	a.	12.09	13.09		14.09	15.09	16.09	17.09	17.37

Mondays to Saturdays

WATERFORD P	d.	18.10	19.10		20.10	21.10		22.31
DUNGARVAN FP	d.	18.24	19.22		20.22	21.22		22.43
YOUGHAL P	a.	18.33	19.32		20.32	21.32		22.53
YOUGHAL P	d.	18.36	19.34		20.34	21.34		22.56
AGHADA FP	d.	18.49	19.47		20.50	21.47		23.09
GOLEEN BRIDGE FP	d.	18.56	19.54		20.57	21.55		
MIDLETON FP	d.	19.01	19.59		21.02	22.01		
GORTACRUE FP	d.	19.04	20.02		21.05	22.06		
CARRIGTWOHILL FP	a.	19.11	20.09		21.12	22.13		

Mondays to Saturdays

CARRIGTWOHILL FP	d.	11.47	12.47	13.47			14.47			15.47
GORTACRUE FP	d.	11.53	12.53	13.53		14.28	14.53	15.03	15.03	15.53
MIDLETON FP	d.	11.56	12.56	13.56			14.56	15.06	15.06	15.56
GOLEEN BRIDGE FP	d.	12.01	13.01	14.01		14.36	15.01	15.13	15.13	16.01
AGHADA FP	d.	12.08	13.08	14.08	14.17	14.44	15.08	15.21	15.21	16.08
YOUGHAL P	a.	12.23	13.23	14.23	14.33	14.59	15.23	15.36	15.36	16.23
YOUGHAL P	d.	12.27	13.27	14.27		14.39	15.27	15.40	15.45	16.27
DUNGARVAN FP	d.	12.35	13.35	14.35		14.47	15.35	15.48	15.53	16.35
WATERFORD P	a.	12.46	13.46	14.46		14.59	15.49	16.00	16.08	16.48

Mondays to Saturdays

CARRIGTWOHILL FP	d.	17.17	17.47	18.11	18.47	19.47		20.47		22.02	23.47
GORTACRUE FP	d.	17.23	17.53	18.17	18.53	19.53		20.53	21.22	22.08	23.53
MIDLETON FP	d.	17.26	17.56	18.20	18.56	19.56		20.56	21.25	22.11	
GOLEEN BRIDGE FP	d.	17.31	18.01	18.25	19.01	20.01		21.01	21.32	22.16	00.01
AGHADA FP	d.	17.38	18.08	18.32	19.08	20.08		21.08	21.39	22.23	00.08
YOUGHAL P	a.	17.53	18.23	18.48	19.23	20.23		21.23	21.53	22.38	00.22
YOUGHAL P	d.	17.57	18.27	18.47	19.27	20.27		21.27	21.58	22.42	
DUNGARVAN FP	d.	18.05	18.35		19.35	20.35		21.35	22.06		
WATERFORD P	a.	18.16	18.46	19.09	19.46	20.48		21.49	22.18	23.00	

Notes:
A Saturdays 15 July to 26 August only.
B Saturdays 8 July to 2 September only.
C Saturdays 27 May to 16 September only.
D Saturdays 20 May to 16 September only.
E 11 June to 3 September only.
F 14 May to 15 October only.
G 20 May to 3 September only.

J Saturdays 10 June to 2 September only.
K Saturdays 27 May to 23 September only.
L 27 May to 2 September only.
M Fridays 26 May and 16 June to 22 September only.
N From 22 October.
S Saturdays only.

CARRIGTWOHILL   MIDLETON   AGHADA   DUNGARVAN

GORTACRUE   GOLEEN BRIDGE   YOUGHAL   WATERFORD

Write in your folder the earliest train and bus connection you can catch to take you to Waterford (remember it's Saturday). Also work out what time you should arrive in Waterford.

Your final task in this unit is to write to your brother to tell him about what happened after you dropped him at the station.

Sean Murphy's experience has probably made you all the more determined to buy a decent second-hand car, so good luck in your search for one.

Unit Nine—You, Your Rights and The Law

'Where ignorance is bliss, 'Tis folly to be wise.'

So says the poet Thomas Gray, but certainly where the law is concerned it is folly to be ignorant. The fact that you didn't know something was wrong is no defence in law so be wise and learn your rights, it could prove helpful. You may also be surprised to learn some of the things you are entitled to do and even more surprised at some of the things you are not entitled to do!

The obvious place to begin is at birth. Others will have to be responsible here for you but you must be registered within twenty-one days of your birth. Usually this is done by either parent if they are married or by your mother if she is not married.

Obviously, if your parent fails to register your birth you will not be entitled to a birth certificate. Think of all the problems you are likely to face later on in life if you don't have a birth certificate.

At Six

You must go to school or receive full-time education. Some parents choose not to send their children to school because they worry about them being bullied or having to obey unnecessary rules, so they arrange to educate them at home. Many of you will claim that you hate school and that you wish your parents had arranged to educate you elsewhere but think about it carefully. Apart from the pleasure you may get from tormenting your teacher can you think of any advantages to the school system?

With more people having access to home computers, much of what you learn at school could be learnt from a computer, but are there any valuable aspects of school life which would be lost if you were to be taught at home?

Try to think up at least four arguments in favour of being educated at school and four arguments in favour of being educated at home.

Organise a class discussion. Listen to what others in your group have to say and then vote in favour of whichever system you think works best.

At Fourteen

You can work part-time during the school year and also during the school holidays. You may only work for a limited number of hours and you are only allowed to do certain types of work. Your employer must get written permission from your parents before offering you work.

Many of you will probably argue that with unemployment being so high if you are lucky enough to be offered a job you should be able to take it. It is easy to see that it would benefit an employer as obviously s/he wouldn't have to pay you the same wages s/he would have to pay an adult. Are there any advantages for you in accepting work at fourteen? Remember that you have your whole working life ahead of you so think carefully before committing yourself.

At Fifteen

1. You can leave school. You are probably breathing a sigh of relief here and dreaming of the bonfire you will make of your copies and other school books. Think of the joy of not having to wear your school uniform again and of never having to miss a favourite television programme because you've got homework to do. Freedom at last! Wait a minute, though. *The Department of Labour School Leavers' Survey shows that those pupils who stay at school to take their Leaving Certificate increase their employment prospects by over 100% compared with early school-leavers with lesser or no qualifications. Think carefully before deciding to leave school.*

What are the advantages for you if you leave at fifteen? Many people believe that fifteen is far too young to leave school and they would like to see the school-leaving age raised to at least sixteen and preferably to seventeen. What do you think of this idea?

You have been elected to represent your school at a meeting with the Minister for Education in the Dail.

- Prepare a three-minute speech explaining why you think the school-leaving age should be raised.

- Be prepared to answer any questions you may be asked.

- Record your speech on a tape recorder and listen to it carefully. Try to sound convinced and decisive.

2. You can work full-time but you are not allowed to work between 10 p.m. and 8 a.m. Why?

3. You can go into a pub but you may not buy alcohol. Bear in mind that the manager/owner of the pub still has the right to refuse you admission.

At Sixteen

1. You can get a licence for a motorcycle of 150 cc or less.

2. You can get a student flying licence.

3. You can buy cigarettes. You are legally entitled to smoke cigarettes at any age but you can't buy cigarettes until you are sixteen.

4. You can get married if your parents/guardians consent to it.

5. You can change your name if your parents/guardians consent to it.

6. You can consent to medical treatment.

7. You can be thrown out of home! Your parents/guardians must maintain you until your sixteenth birthday. So remember don't push your luck too far. Don't treat your home like a hotel or before you know it you might get notice to quit!

At Seventeen

1. You can get a provisional driving licence.

2. You can join the defence forces.

3. You can hold a private air pilot's licence.

4. You can be sent to prison depending on your crime. A male juvenile offender aged between fifteen and nineteen may also be sent to St Patrick's Institution: there is no equivalent institution for females.

There are a number of different types of courts in Ireland. Different courts deal with different levels of crime. Cases against children and young people under seventeen are heard by a District Justice in a **Children's Court**. Members of the public are not allowed to attend sessions of the Children's Court.

5. If you are a woman you may have sexual intercourse. It is **statutory rape** for a male to have sexual intercourse with a female who is under seventeen. It doesn't matter whether the female is willing, it is still rape. The only exception is if the female marries at sixteen with her parents/guardians' consent, then she may have sexual intercourse with her husband.

At Eighteen

1. You can claim benefits such as unemployment and supplementary welfare allowance.

2. You can drive a motorcycle over 150 cc and drive heavy trucks.*

3. You can hold a commercial air pilot's licence.*

4. You can sit on a jury.*

5. You can vote.

6. You can drink alcohol in a pub although the management still has the right to refuse to serve you.

7. You can place a bet with a bookmaker.

8. You can leave home.

9. You can sign a contract.

10. You can change your name without your parents/guardians' consent. On 12 September 1984, a daughter was born to Mr and Mrs Williams in Texas. They blessed her with the name Rhoshandiateblyneshiaunne Veshenk Royaanfsquatsiuty. Perhaps you would like to change yours to something similar!

11. You can be a blood donor and donate organs for transplant.

12. You can stand for election to the local council.

13. You can get a passport without your parents/guardians' consent.

You will notice that some of your rights have been marked with an asterisk. Do you think that it is rather strange that you can literally take people's lives in your hands (drive heavy trucks and hold an air pilot's licence) and you can also make decisions about the future of other people by sitting on a jury and yet you still cannot marry without your parents/guardians' consent?

- Do you think that some of the rights so far listed are unreasonable?

- Would you change the age limit of any of them? If you would—which ones would you change and why?

- Discuss your rights with your partner and then draw up your own charter. Do be realistic and reasonable. If you want to be treated like an adult you must prove that you can behave in a responsible fashion.

At Twenty-one

1. You can get married without your parents/guardians' consent.

2. You can hold a licence to sell alcohol.

3. You can stand for election to Dail Eireann.

4. You can drive a large passenger vehicle and all heavy goods vehicles.

5. You can run a gaming shop.

At what age can you do the following?

THE LAW	AGE
Change your name without your parents' consent	
Buy alcohol in a pub	
Buy cigarettes	
Leave school	
Vote	
Sell alcohol	
Drive a heavy truck	
Leave home	
Stand for election to the local council	
Hold a private air pilot's licence	

Now that you know so many of your rights you will probably want to find out what other rights you have: there is still much for you to find out. No doubt there are many other teenagers who don't know their rights either. Your task is to inform them.

First of all, try to find out information about your other rights. Information should be available from:

- Library
- Citizens' Advice Bureaux
- Youth services
- Garda stations.

Then write your own booklet aimed at teenagers telling them what their legal rights are. From your own experience you will know that a long-winded legal document would not interest them so make your booklet informative, interesting and concise.

- Use graphics and cartoons to help you.

- Try to think up an appropriate title for your booklet.

- Design a cover for your booklet which is both eye-catching and relevant.

Maybe your booklet will be so successful that you could even consider selling it to youth groups and other teenagers, donating the proceeds to the Irish Society for the Prevention of Cruelty to Children (I.S.P.C.C.).

Apart from the specific rights mentioned, you have other rights which you should know about. Some young people, especially perhaps in the cities, often feel that the Gardai are always picking on them and harassing them. This is unlikely to be the case as they are far too busy dealing with genuine crimes to bother wasting either their time or your time. However, there may be exceptions.

So what are your rights here? The Gardai do not have the power to stop and question you except when they have reasonable grounds to suspect you of having committed an offence or of being about to commit an offence. Even if you really feel that they have no reason to stop you, remember they're the ones with the power so be polite and patient. *Don't* antagonise them, you're likely to be the loser.

If the Gardai do decide to arrest you, remember you still have rights.

You *must* go with them to the Garda Station. You will be allowed to make one telephone call.

The Gardai are not allowed to question anyone under the age of seventeen unless there is an independent adult present to represent the young person. This is usually a parent or relative but any adult not connected with the Gardai will do.

The Gardai also have the right to stop and search you if they have reasonable grounds to suspect that you may be carrying drugs. Obviously, when we talk about drugs here, we don't mean a packet of Hedex or a bottle of cough medicine. We are talking about controlled substances such as heroin, cannabis, ecstasy, etc. The Gardai may search you on the street or they may ask you to go with them to the Garda Station. You *must* go even if you know that you're not carrying anything illegal. If you refuse to allow them to search you or if you refuse to go to the Station with them, you can be charged with obstruction.

Elsewhere in this book you will have learned that there is a difference between **assertion** and **aggression**. If you feel that the Gardai are treating you unfairly, then do speak out but be assertive not aggressive. Look up the meanings of these words.

Working with a partner, prepare two scenes to act out to the rest of the class. In each scene, you have been stopped by the Gardai.

1. In Scene 1 you respond aggressively.

2. In Scene 2 you respond assertively.

Discuss the differences in the way you behaved. Decide which of your reactions was most effective.

You have the right to grow in health, safety and opportunity. You have the right to grow free from the fear of physical abuse, sexual abuse and neglect.

 A United Nation's Declaration states that 'Mankind Owes to the Child the Best it has to Give'.

Sadly, for many children, the best that they are given is nowhere near good enough.

Parents are the natural guardians of their children. They are responsible for their care. However, the 'right' that parents believe they have to control and discipline their children is based more on social and moral pressures than on law.

In the past it was believed that parents and guardians of children had the right to beat their children. Many adults believed that it was not just a right but their duty to physically discipline their children. They were able to quote the *Bible* to support their case. The *Bible* says 'He that spareth his rod hateth his son' or as Samuel Butler puts it 'Spare the rod, and spoil the child'.

What do you think of the above two statements? Are there any occasions on which you think it is right to hit a child?

Some of you are going to say that there is a big difference between giving a child a smack on its bottom and beating it with a stick. The problem is where does one draw the line? Obviously, it is not acceptable to beat a child with a stick, but is it acceptable to hit a child around the head?

Would it be better to say that physical punishment is a form of degrading treatment and that adults who have the advantage of being physically stronger should not have the right to hit a child? The abuse and neglect of any child is a cause for concern because not only do children suffer at the time but they often grow up to repeat the same parenting pattern with their own children. In other words, a battered child may become a battering parent.

Organise a formal discussion on the idea that 'to spare the rod is to spoil the child'. If, after your discussion, you decide that you would ban all physical punishment decide how you would go about letting people know.

Plan a national campaign using posters, local radio and television broadcasts. Remember this is an emotive issue. Parents will not like the idea that anyone should tell them how to treat their children, however children should/must come first, so be firm, decisive but sensitive.

In the past, in Sweden, parents and guardians of children had the right to beat their children. The law of 1920 relating to children born in wedlock said that parents had the right to 'punish' their children. However, in 1949, the word 'punish' was replaced by the word 'reprimand'.

- Punish—to cause one to suffer, to beat.

- Reprimand—a severe reproof or telling off.

In 1966, the right of parents to beat their children was removed. This means that if a parent strikes her/his child, the act is judged in the same way as if the parent had beaten another adult or beaten someone else's children. Do you think that the time has come for other countries to follow Sweden's example?

You have the right to grow free from the fear of sexual abuse.

In recent years, many children have been the victims of sexual abuse. It is not that sexual abuse of children didn't happen in the past but we are becoming more aware of the lasting damage such abuse can cause to children. Research has shown that 10% of under-eighteens suffer some form of mild or serious abuse. About 3% of under-eighteens suffer serious sexual abuse. Studies have shown that a sexually abused child can become a sexually abusing adult.

Often young people will know more about what is happening to their friends than an adult will. If you believe that someone you know is being sexually/physically abused, you *must* do something about it. There are people you can turn to who will treat what you have to say in confidence. If you feel that you cannot talk to anyone you know, then you should ring **Childline**.

Design a leaflet explaining the work of Childline and giving their telephone number. Do not be sensationalist. Thousands of Irish children are suffering untold misery as a result of such abuse. Your leaflet should be informative, it should not frighten or alarm. Treat this matter sensitively.

There is absolutely no excuse for the abuse or neglect of children. Adults who mistreat children should have their children taken from them so that they cannot repeat the abuse.

However, it is not only the abuser who is to blame. We must share the blame for allowing such things to happen. Perhaps there were times when we could have helped but didn't. Maybe we felt afraid to interfere. Read the poem 'Saw it in the papers' by Adrian Mitchell.

What is the poet trying to say?

Do you agree with him?

Can you feel any sympathy for the woman?

Saw it in the papers

I will not say her name
Because I believe she hates her name.

But there was this woman who lived in Yorkshire.

Her baby was two years old.
She left him, strapped in his pram, in the kitchen.
She went out.
She stayed with friends.
She went out drinking.

The baby was hungry.
Nobody came.
The baby cried.
Nobody came.

The baby tore at the upholstery of his pram.
Nobody came.
She told the police:
'I thought the neighbours would hear him crying,
and report it to someone who would come
and take him away.'

Nobody came.

The baby died of hunger.

She said she'd arranged for a girl,
Whose name she couldn't remember,
To come and look after the baby
While she stayed with friends.
Nobody saw the girl.
Nobody came.

Her lawyer said there was no evidence
of mental instability.
But the man who promised to marry her
Went off with another woman.

And when he went off, this mother changed
from a mother who cared for her two-year-old baby
into a mother who did not seem to care at all.
There was no evidence of mental instability.

The Welfare Department spokesman said:
'I do not know of any plans for an inquiry.
We never became deeply involved.'
Nobody came.
There was no evidence of mental instability.

When she was given love
She gave love freely to her baby.
When love was torn away from her
she locked her love away.
It seemed that no one cared for her.
She seemed to stop caring.
Nobody came.
There was no evidence of mental instability.

Only love can unlock locked-up-love.

Manslaughter: She pleaded Guilty.
She was sentenced to be locked up
In prison for four years.

Is there any love in prisons?

She must have been in great pain.

Now she is locked up.
There is love in prisons,
But it is all locked up.

What she did to him was terrible.
There was no evidence of mental instability.
What we are doing to her is terrible.
There is no evidence of mental instability.

Millions of children starve, but not in England.
What we do not do for them is terrible.

Is England's love locked up in England?
There is no evidence of mental instability.

Only love can unlock locked-up love.

When I read about it in the papers I cried.
When my friend read about it in the papers he cried.
We shared our tears.
They did not help her at all.

She has been locked up
For locking up her love.
There was no evidence of mental instability.

Unlock all of your love.
You have enough to feed all those millions of children.
Unlock all of your love.
You have enough for this woman.

Cry if you like.
Do something if you can. You can.

Unlock your love and send it to this woman.
I am sending her my love.

—Adrian Mitchell

Unit Ten—Consumer Affairs and Assertiveness

We all have duties, rights and responsibilities. There should be justice and fair play for all. In terms of consumer law and consumer protection, the Office of Consumer Affairs tries to ensure this justice and fair play. When you pay money for goods and services you should expect value for money. As you have worked hard for your money there is absolutely no reason why you should be sold shoddy goods.

A **consumer** is a person who uses goods, products or services. When you buy a newspaper or a loaf of bread at your local shop you are the consumer of a **product**.

When you use the Dart rail service or go to the theatre you are the consumer of a **service**.

From the list below show whether you are buying a Product or a Service.

washing machine	litre of milk
shoes	cinema
restaurant meal	newspaper
library	coal
ferry	plumber
drycleaning	launderette

There is a well-known Latin phrase *Caveat Emptor* which means 'Let the buyer beware'. This obviously means that you, as the consumer, must exercise common sense and carefully examine goods before purchase.

In the past a consumer had very few rights if goods purchased turned out to be faulty. Now, however, there is a great improvement in the situation. Consumers now have legal protection. A vital piece of legislation was introduced in 1980. This act is called 'The Sale of Goods and Supply of Services Act 1980'.

When you buy goods you are in fact entering into a contract with the seller. Under this contract you have *four* main entitlements:

1. That goods must be of **merchantable quality**.

2. The goods must be **reasonably fit for the particular purpose** for which the buyer intends to use them.

3. The goods must be **as described**.

4. If goods are bought on seeing a sample, the goods **must conform to the sample**.

These four main entitlements are very important so we will examine them in greater detail.

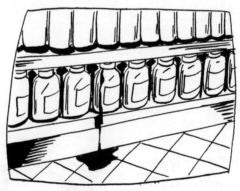

Merchantable Quality.   Goods must be fit to be bought. If a product cannot be used for its normal purpose it is not of merchantable quality. If you buy a tumble dryer, and it does not work, or if you buy a frozen chicken and it is rotten, or if you buy a pair of shoes which come apart at the seams when you first wear them—well, none of these goods, obviously, is of merchantable quality.

Fitness for the Intended Purpose.   If you buy a can opener—it should open cans.

If you tell the shop owner/retailer that you require a very strong spade for gardening—then this is what you should get. The retailer should be reasonably knowledgeable about the goods s/he is selling. Therefore, if the spade snaps in two the first time you use it you have a right to assume that the spade was not fit for the intended purpose. You should be entitled to a full refund or a proper replacement.

Goods Must be as Described.   A retailer should not describe goods in a false or misleading way. In advertisements, words and pictures should accurately reflect what is being sold. Therefore, if you buy a washing powder with 'suitable for woollens' written on it and this powder ruins your woollens, then you have the right to complain and to seek redress from the retailer as the goods were not **as described**.

Unfortunately false and misleading advertising is all too common today. It is a clichéd joke at this stage to talk of a second-hand car dealer advertising a car as having had 'one careful owner', but forgetting to mention the many careless ones.

24-Hour Service often isn't quite that! Holiday brochures often promise that apartments are only two minutes from the beach when in reality it could be a twenty-minute walk. Often a rainproof anorak is anything but rainproof.

Goods Must Conform to Sample. When goods are bought based on seeing a sample, e.g. wallpaper, material, carpet etc., the goods should conform to the sample.

You know now what rights you have regarding faulty goods. But who should you approach to rectify the situation when a problem arises? In nearly all cases the responsibility lies with the seller as it is the seller who has made the contract with the buyer. So you must contact the retailer of the goods without delay.

Some retailers try to give the impression that the consumer/buyer does not have certain rights under 'The Sale of Goods and Supply of Services Act 1980', by putting the following notices in their shops:

This, however, is *not* acceptable. In fact a trader who uses these statements may be committing an offence. It is wrong for a trader to attempt to limit a consumer's legal rights.

Naturally, a retailer has rights also. S/he cannot be held responsible for defects which arise through misuse of the goods by the consumer. If you buy an electric razor and use it for shearing sheep, you really can't expect the retailer to take your complaint seriously when the razor breaks down.

Also, you can't justifiably complain if you bought a leather jacket and you discover the next day that you could have bought it cheaper in another shop. When you feel that you have a genuine complaint you should report the problem immediately to the retailer. You may be entitled to a full refund if, for example, the washing machine you bought never worked. You could be entitled to a part refund or repair if you have used the goods for a while before they break down, or if you delayed reporting the damage.

It is regrettable but traders often will try and insist that you accept a credit note instead of a full cash refund. Remember, if your complaint is justified you can refuse all offers of credit notes and insist on cash. Even if you buy goods in a sale the same rules apply, unless you have been informed that the goods are of inferior quality or 'seconds'.

You cannot however expect second-hand goods to be as good as new ones but they must still be fit for their purpose and of reasonable quality. So if you save up your hard-earned money and buy a second-hand car for £3,650, it must be in good order.

If you are not satisfied with the goods you have purchased then you may complain initially in three ways:

☞ *In person*

☞ *By letter*

☞ *By telephone.*

Write out two advantages and two disadvantages of **each** of these methods.

Read carefully the article 'Tips on how to complain', from *Consumer Choice* magazine.

You worked hard during the summer holidays and then treated yourself to a pair of expensive runners. When you first wore them they started to fall apart. You were very annoyed as they cost you £65 and you wanted to wear them that weekend at the sports camp. When you complained in person you were not taken seriously by the shop assistant, so your next step is to write to the shopowner.

Using the sample letter opposite as a guide, write a letter of complaint giving all relevant details:

- The item purchased.
- Date and price of purchase.
- Problem which arose.
- What action should be taken.

Choice COUNSEL

TEN TIPS ON HOW TO COMPLAIN

✔ Ask yourself what you want to achieve. Complaining involves a lot of hassle—worthwhile if you get your money back. But with some complaints, you can expect no more than an apology (and perhaps a better deal for the next customer).

✔ Know your rights. But don't be too quick to quote them—the light touch might get a better result.

✔ Complain as soon as possible. Getting your rights requires prompt action.

✔ Complain to the right person. Don't vent your anger on the cashier or the telephonist—ask to see the manager (or whoever is in charge). Keep a note of their name and address, and always write to or telephone them personally.

✔ Complain in person. A personal visit often succeeds where a letter or phone call doesn't. But keep it friendly—don't lose your temper.

✔ Follow up in writing. Type (or write legibly), setting out the following: the facts of the purchase—what you bought, when, and what you paid, the nature of your complaint, the legal position as you see it, what you wish done about it (e.g. a refund, immediate action or whatever).
Enclose copies (not originals) of relevant documents such as bills, sales literature and so on. Sending the letter by registered post (95p extra) may make a greater impact and gives you proof of receipt.

Letter of complaint

Dear Sir/Madam

On 9 June 1988 I bought a Kabashi video cassette recorder K43 model from your shop (copy of receipt attached).

From the beginning, I had difficulty in ejecting cassettes. Ten days after the purchase, a cassette jammed solidly, and the unit no longer operates.

Under the Sale of Goods and Supply of Services Act 1980, goods sold should be of merchantable quality. The premature failure of the video recorder shows there was an inherent fault at the time of purchase, and it was not of merchantable quality.

Relying on the Sale of Goods Acts, I therefore reject the goods and expect to receive the full purchase price of £429.50. Please also arrange to collect the recorder at your convenience, and within 14 days of the date on this letter.

I look forward to hearing from you.

Your faithfully

Notes
Use precise name

State purchase and give details of model

State the problem

Ask for satisfaction

Ask for action within a reasonable time

Enclose copies (not originals)

✔ Keep the paperwork. Never throw away anything that might be relevant. Keep copies of all letters, notes of phone calls and visits, and anything else which might help.

✔ Stick at it. Don't lose patience—some of the successful complaints take a year or more to sort out. And don't let traders fob you off with less than your rights. (On the other hand, be ready to call it a day if you get a reasonable offer or you reach a dead end—know when to cut your losses).

✔ Don't be afraid to ask for help. If direct negotiation fails, there may sometimes be a

third party, such as a trade association, Office of Consumer Affairs and Fair Trade (false descriptions), or other group, which might be able to offer assistance in the case of goods and services. As a last resort, however, if you believe you have a legal right which the trader refuses to recognise, you may have to consider seeking legal advice or taking legal action. It is normally only a court which can require a seller to give compensation if the seller does not wish to do so.

✔ Give praise where it's due. Saying thank you not only helps keep good services good—it also builds up goodwill for when something goes wrong.

Small Claims Courts are a recent significant development in consumer law and consumer protection. These are organised through the District Court Offices. At the moment the Small Claims Courts are operating on a pilot/experimental basis in Dublin, Cork and Sligo. There is a limit of £500 compensation at these courts.

If you don't get any satisfaction from the retailer, but do not wish to take your complaint to the Small Claims Court, then you should seek help from the Office of Consumer Affairs and Fair Trade, or the Consumer Association of Ireland. You could also seek the assistance of the State's Ombudsman, currently Mr Michael Mills. The Office of the Ombudsperson deals with all types of problems—from mistakes in ESB and telephone bills to problems with faulty goods.

When a person feels that s/he has in some way been 'conned' it is not unusual for this person to feel quite angry. This anger should not be allowed to turn into aggression as this could be counter-productive—you might make things worse not better.

There is a world of difference between being **aggressive** and being **assertive**.

> **Aggression** is *negative*
>
> **Assertion** is *positive*

Assertiveness is being able to express your thoughts, ideas, opinions, feelings and needs openly, clearly and directly without putting yourself or others down.

It is about resolving conflicts and differences of opinion in a way that leaves both parties feeling good about themselves, even if they do not have all their needs met by the outcome.

Assertiveness is about respecting yourself and other people. It is not simply aimed at getting what you want if getting what you want means trampling over the needs of others.

It is about standing up for your rights but this does not mean that you can violate the rights of others.

Aggressiveness involves expressing your feelings and opinions but in a way that threatens or puts down the other person. The aim is to get your own way no matter what.

People who are aggressive in discussion are often very sarcastic and hurtful.

Non-Assertiveness involves hoping that you will get what you want but leaving it to chance or to another person to guess what it is you want. You don't want to upset anyone so you avoid asking directly for what you really want.

The drawings below should help to illustrate the difference between assertiveness, aggression and non-assertiveness.

Aggressive *My needs are more important than yours.*

Non-Assertive *Your needs are more important than mine.*

Assertive *We both have needs. Both our needs are important. You tell me yours. I'll tell you mine. Then we can see what we can work out between us.*

When you are assertive you can feel good about yourself because you have been open and honest. When you feel good about yourself you gain confidence and you feel less anxious and frustrated. Being assertive can, of course, come in very handy when you wish to make a complaint, but, far more important is the fact that when you are assertive—when you can express your feelings openly to another person—you increase your chances of getting the kind of relationship you want, the friends you want, and the job you want.

Many personal relationships are doomed because neither party is open or honest. Perhaps there are times when you feel unable to express your needs, desires and feelings. You hope that your friend/partner will instinctively know what it is that you really want. Unfortunately, most of us are not mind readers, so if you do not express a preference you can hardly blame your friend/partner for making a choice which suits her/him.

When this happens you feel resentful. This resentment will build up inside you and eventually you will explode in anger. This whole situation is totally unnecessary—all that was needed was for you to say what you wanted and your friend to say what s/he wanted.

If you both wanted different things any unpleasantness could have been avoided if you had discussed the situation openly and reached a compromise. Remember, no relationship can succeed if one partner is a door mat and the other a bully.

If asserting ourselves is such a good thing why then are so many people afraid or reluctant to do so?

There are many reasons for this:

- As small children we were praised for being good—for doing what others wanted us to do. We all like to be praised so we believe that people will like us if we do what they want.

- Some cultures and religions strongly discourage assertiveness, e.g. the traditional Christian teaching—'turn the other cheek'. There is also an idea that it is in someway not 'ladylike' to be assertive.

- Schools often reward the quiet, obedient child whilst sometimes viewing the curious child with many opinions, and the desire to express these opinions, as being in some way disruptive.

- Sometimes you may not be sure about your rights.

As we have said there are many reasons why people find it difficult to be assertive, but there are skills which you can learn which can make it much easier for you.

Assertiveness Skills

- Knowing your rights.

- Knowing what you want and saying it clearly.

- Saying 'I'.

- Looking the person in the eye.

- Being open, direct and honest.

- Listening.

- Using the broken record technique.

The aim of the 'broken record' technique is to make your needs known to another person without getting angry or loud when the other person is trying to side-track you or avoid hearing what you are saying.

If for example you return a faulty food mixer to a shop, before you approach the retailer:

- Be sure about your rights.

- Identify exactly what you want (refund/repair).

- Decide on a clear, simple statement.

When you are speaking to the retailer repeat the statement calmly and confidently, i.e. 'I want a full refund on this item' after every response which does not solve the problem. You can acknowledge the 'red herring' or side issues but do not respond to them. Then repeat the statement. You must remain calm—the effect is boring and exhausting and the retailer should decide to co-operate if only to stop the record.

Read the following dialogue:

Customer   *I bought this food mixer here last week. It never worked. I've had it checked out—the motor is faulty. I want a full cash refund on this item please.*

Retailer   *Really, well I've been in business a long time and nobody else has ever made such a complaint.*

Customer   *Indeed, however, the motor is faulty. I want a refund on this item.*

Retailer   *We have sold hundreds of this particular motor. We never had one which was faulty.*

Customer   *That's interesting, but this one is faulty and I want a full refund.*

Retailer   *This is our most popular brand, it's always in demand.*

Customer   *That may well be the case, but this food mixer does not work so I want a full refund.*

Retailer   *Are you sure you read the instructions properly? Perhaps you damaged it by using it incorrectly.*

Customer   *Yes, I read the instructions. This machine is faulty. I want a full refund on my money.*

This technique is very useful and generally successful when:

- You know your rights.

- You feel strongly enough to be persistent.

- The person you are making the request of is awkward or manipulative.

Using role play, practise making a request assertively, using the 'broken-record' technique.

Think of a situation of your own or use one of the following:

- Ask your neighbour to do her/his D.I.Y. at a reasonable hour. It's 12.15 a.m. and you can't sleep with all the noise.

- Ask a shopkeeper to give you your money back for the bread you bought yesterday which was mouldy.

Assertiveness is not just about the ability to express negative feelings like annoyance and hurt, nor is it just about standing up for your rights—in making complaints, refusing requests and refusing to be put down. Assertiveness is also about expressing positive feelings.

This is a most rewarding aspect of assertiveness—as we can:

- Express affection

- Give compliments

- Receive compliments

- Ask for help

- Initiate conversations

- Express appreciation.

Now that you have learned how to be assertive and to express your feelings directly, there will be no more long nights lying in bed seething in anger about the fight you had with your friend and thinking about all the remarks you should have made. This type of situation will no longer arise. You know how to express your feelings and how to enable your friend to do likewise.

Remember what Shakespeare said:
'To Thine Own Self Be True'.

Unit Eleven—Language

Words . . . Words . . . Words

The English language is a living language. It is constantly changing. New words are added as necessary, old ones are discarded when they are no longer needed. Words change their form, pronounciation and even their meaning to meet the ever changing needs of people. 'Old English' is the foundation of the English language. This was used by the Romans, Anglo Saxons and the Jutes. The Vikings and Normans brought further changes. The English language became more varied still during the Renaissance around 1500.

The renewed interest in classical literature introduced many Latin and Greek words into the English language. Modern English is what has emerged from this.

The Irish language has further enriched the English spoken in Ireland today. Irish idioms, vocabulary and structure are to be found in everyday use, e.g. 'I met Sean and I going down the road', 'I'm after eating my breakfast'.

Many words have their origins in the Irish language:

☞   *Brogue, galore, gombeen*

☞   *Smithereens, leprechaun, boreen, poteen.*

Much of the dialogue in J. M. Synge's plays is, in fact, direct translation from Gaelic, e.g.

Maurya: *'In the big world the old people do be leaving things after them for their sons and children, but in this place it is the young men do be leaving things behind for them that do be old.'*

From *Riders to the Sea*

The origins of the English language are very varied—in fact it would be fair to say that if the English language were a dog it would be a mongrel!

Language is made up of words. It is vital that you spell these words correctly. Very often, poor spelling is caused by neglect—by not making any effort. You must begin by noticing words. You must look at the word and take a 'mental photograph'. When you have a correct mental picture of a word, you will find it easier to recognise a word which is spelt incorrectly.

There is no easy way to become good at spelling. Like most things in life, if you make the effort you will get good results.

Remember:

 It is never too late to improve your spelling.

Your spelling will improve greatly if you:

- Look at words carefully—*notice* words.

- Be aware of *danger points* for spelling.

- *Memorise* the correct way to spell words.

- Always, when in any doubt, *use a dictionary.*

You will feel much more confident in writing letters, answering advertisements, applying for jobs once you have mastered the art of spelling words correctly.

The words which follow are among the most commonly *misspelt*.

A

Address
Amount
Argue
Argument
Author
Athlete
Accommodation
Anxious
Assistant
Autumn
Across
Achieve
Aerial
Appoint
Association
Awkward

B

Beautiful
Biscuit
Build
Business
Beginning
Begin
Benefit

C

Ceiling
Conscious
Chimney
Conscience
Committee
Condemn

D

Deceive
Disappoint
Dissatisfied
Disappear
Description
Describe
Definitely

E

Existence
Eerie
Exceed
Except
Embarrass

F

February
Forty

G

Grammar
Grief

H

Holiday
Height
Humour

I

Immediately
Insistent
Independent

J

Judge
Judgement/judgment

K

Knowledge
Knowledgeable

L

Library
Likeable
Length
Leisure
Lovable

M

Marriage
Maintenance
Maintain
Mischievous
Mischief
Murmur

N

Necessary
Ninety
Neighbour
Noticeable
Niece

O

Occur
Occurrence
Organiser

P

Parallel
Privilege
Possess
Panic
Poem
Panicking
Poetry

Q

Queue
Queuing

R

Receive
Restaurant
Receipt
Ridiculous
Recommend

S

Secretary
Succeed
Success
Separate
Sincere
Surprise
Similar
Sincerely

T

True
Theatre
Truly
Thorough

U

Umbrella

V

Vicious
View
Vegetable

W

Wednesday
Wholly
Weird
Whole

Y

Yacht
Yield

Task

- Examine the words given.

- Memorise/learn off the correct spelling.

- Rewrite the words into your folder.

- Set yourself a target, e.g. to learn ten per week during the year.

- Revise.

Apart from misspelling words, it is very easy to confuse words which have a *similar sound* but *different meaning*. There are so many of these (**homonyms**) in the English language that the confusion is understandable.

Homonyms are words which have a similar sound but a different meaning.

Heard	—	I *heard* the music
Herd	—	A *herd* of cattle
Waist	—	*Part of the body*
Waste	—	*What is left over, to misuse*

Write *short* sentences, one for each word, showing the correct use of the following:

Hire—Higher	*Principle—Principal*
Stake—Steak	*To—Too—Two*
Their—There	*Stationary—Stationery*
Bored—Board	*Muscle—Mussel*
Whole—Hole	

Rewrite the sentences below, inserting the correct word in the appropriate space:

(*aloud, allowed*)

It is not _____ to speak _____ in class.

(*sale, sail*)

The yacht is for _____ complete with a new _____ .

(*piece, peace*)

There will be no _____ until the toddler gets a _____ of cake.

(*wait, weight*)

I had to _____ to check if I got the correct _____ .

(*seen, scene*)

I have never _____ a _____ like that before.

(*pane, pain*)

He was in _____ when he put his head through a _____ of glass.

Look now at **synonyms** and **antonyms**.

Synonyms are words which are similar in meaning.

Accused	—	*Blamed*
Disaster	—	*Calamity*
Enemy	—	*Foe*
Quantity	—	*Amount*

1. Give synonyms for the following:

Modern	*Fear*
Famous	*Regret*
Strong	*Cheat*
Exterior	*Wicked*
Empty	*Abandon*

2. Arrange the following list of words in groups of *three* synonyms:

Residence	Surrender	Phantom
Illness	Skinny	Malady
Fast	Abode	Yield
Forsake	Ghost	Dwelling
Give up	Spirit	Lean
Leave	Thin	Disease
Quick	Desert	Rapid

Antonyms are words opposite in meaning to another word.

Bitter — Sweet

Success — Failure

Match each word in the list on the left with its antonym in the list on the right:

Permanent	Dark
Bright	Maximum
Clean	Entrance
Deep	Slow
Rapid	Temporary
Straight	Dirty
Exit	Plural
Singular	Crooked
Minimum	Shallow

Apostrophe

The Apostrophe is used:

1. To show possession/ownership.

2. To show where certain letters have been omitted.

People tend to be very careless about the use of the apostrophe. It would seem that many people believe that every word which ends in the letter 's' requires an apostrophe—this is not necessarily the case. Learn the following simple rules and don't commit the 'crime' of misusing the apostrophe.

To show possession/ownership

- Mary's bicycle—means the bicycle belonging to Mary.

- The baby's tooth—means the tooth belonging to the baby.

If the noun is plural and ends in 's', then the apostrophe comes after the 's'—s':

SINGULAR	PLURAL
The bird's egg	The birds' eggs
The teacher's car	The teachers' cars

Remember—for a simple plural, where ownership is not involved, do not add an apostrophe, e.g. boxes, sweets, chips, chairs.

To show where certain letters have been omitted

- It's—it is

- Can't—cannot

- O'clock—of the clock

- Won't—will not

- Haven't—have not

Note:

it's = it is

Its (no apostrophe) means 'of it'—the cat chased its tail. To write 'the cat chased it's tail' would not make sense, as it would read 'the cat chased it is tail'.

> twould be nice to be
> an apostrophe
> floating
> above an s
> hovering
> like a paper kite
> in between the its
> eavesdropping, tiptoeing
> high above the thats
> an inky comet
> spiralling
> the highest tossed
> off hats
>
> *Roger McGough*

The following notices were seen in shops, restaurants and on roadways:

- Look at each sign.

- Where is the mistake?

- Write out the correct version.

Ladie's Hairdresser	*Strawberry Milk Shake's*
Bean's And Chips	*Batchelor's Peas*
Road Work's Ahead	*10 Apple's 90p.*

Language should be used correctly *and* appropriately. Appropriateness (suitability) of language is very important. Obviously, the way you would chat or write to your best friend and the way you would converse with a prospective employer at an interview would be very different.

You would, of course, speak or write to a friend in an informal, friendly way. Whereas, when you write to an employer, you adopt a more business-like, formal tone.

Expressions which are used in everyday conversation, though not in formal situations, are called **colloquialisms**. The word colloquialism comes from the Latin word for conversation.

For example:

To have your heart in your mouth	To be frightened
Dead beat	Totally exhausted
To throw in the towel	Give up the struggle
To sit on the fence	To avoid taking sides
To live from hand to mouth	To live in hardship
To put one's foot in it	To say or do the wrong thing. To cause embarrassment.

Find out where the following expressions originated:

- To throw in the towel (*hint*: boxing)
- To pull out all the stops (*hint*: organ music)

1. Explain what is meant by the following colloquial expressions (if you do not know for certain, use your imagination):

   A wet blanket

   On the level

   A chip off the old block

   In the same boat

   To smell a rat

   To pull one's leg

To let the cat out of the bag

To nip in the bud

To bury the hatchet

Strike while the iron is hot

To have a bee in your bonnet

Give the cold shoulder

Make both ends meet

Haul over the coals

To play with fire

To burn the candle at both ends

At loggerheads

Hit below the belt.

2. Put six of the above colloquialisms into sentences.

3. Write a conversation between two people using colloquial speech.

Slang

Colloquial expressions are accepted in everyday usage. Slang, however, is not accepted in serious speech or writing. Slang is very informal language that includes new and sometimes impolite words and meanings.

For example:

To take a dekko	to look
To cog	to copy
Mot	girlfriend
To mosey around	to roam around
Brill	brilliant
To nick	to steal

Make a list of at least *six* slang words used in everyday speech.

Colloquialisms and slang are often used in everyday situations. However, it would be totally inappropriate to use either in a business letter or at a business meeting.

If your employer asked you to write a report to be read at the firm's Annual General Meeting, you should, of course, write it using the appropriate language and style.

Report Writing

A **Report** is a written statement of the facts of a situation, process or project.

- A garage mechanic might be asked to write a report on the condition of a car.

- The Gardai might ask you to give a statement of what you saw when there was a traffic accident.

- A journalist might report on a public meeting.

Report writing is always necessary in the business world.

Terms Of Reference

When writing a report, you must state the purpose of the report. If you are reporting on the results of market research undertaken, e.g. *Report on result of Market Research Questionnaire for* (name of mini-company), this is called 'defining your Terms of Reference'.

It is important to remember the following when writing a report:

- Reports should be brief and should be simply and clearly expressed.

- Essential information only must be given. The information should not be given in a long-winded style. It should be *concise* and *precise*.

- The contents must be arranged in a sensible and logical order. Section headings and sub-headings help.

- Remember, you must not express personal opinions. You must state the facts, e.g. what was done during the year, what was said at a meeting.

- Sometimes, at the end of your report, you may, if requested, give your own opinion or make recommendations. If doing so, it must be clearly stated that you are expressing your own views.

- Reports must be signed and dated.

Write a concise report on *three* of the following:

- An accident you witnessed.

- Proceedings of your company's Annual General Meeting.

- An exhibition or display you attended.

- A public meeting you attended.

- Leisure facilities for young people in your locality.

- Activities of your Youth Club.

- The damage done to your kitchen after a frying pan caught fire.

Clichés

Unfortunately, our language is littered with clichés. Clichés are expressions which have become stale and almost meaningless through overuse. You must try to avoid the use of clichés or hackneyed expressions in your spoken and written English.

Politicians often use clichés in their speeches, usually because they hope that their audience will be so impressed by the language and style that they will forget about the content—or lack of it. Using clichés is really just a roundabout way of saying little or nothing.

Read the paragraph below:

- What in fact is this politician saying?
- Count the clichés.

> Unemployment is a huge problem in Ireland today. We must root it out, we must cure this cancer in our society, we must leave no stone unturned in our search for a solution. The time has come for all politicians to stand together, to stand up and be counted, to put our noses to the grindstone and our shoulders to the wheel and at all times keep our ears to the ground. It must get top priority on the political agenda. We must seek consensus and have full and frank and meaningful discussion with other politicians and the business community. We must get around the table and discuss this issue at grass roots level. We must grasp the nettle, we must take the problem on board—we are at a crossroads and we must go down the road which leads to full employment. We must not dodge this issue, etc. etc. etc.

Write a similar type paragraph on:

- Education
- The Youth of Ireland
- The Housing Shortage

Proverbs

A **proverb** is a short, well-known, wise saying, expressing a supposed truth or a moral lesson, e.g. a bird in the hand is worth two in the bush.

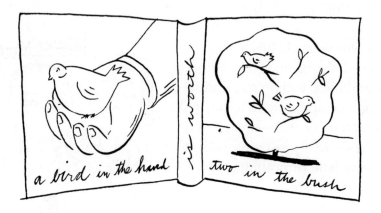

This means that we should look after what we have (the bird in the hand) rather than striving for what we might never achieve.

Most proverbs contain quite a lot of common sense. It has been said that proverbs represent the 'distilled wisdom of the ages'. What do you think this might mean? Look up the meaning of 'distilled' in your dictionary.

What is meant by the following proverbs? Can you imagine how some of them might have originated?

A drowning man will clutch at a straw.

A stitch in time saves nine.

When in Rome do as the Romans do.

One swallow does not make a summer.

Great oaks from little acorns grow.

It's an ill wind that blows nobody any good.

Let not the pot call the kettle black.

One man's meat is another man's poison.

The early bird catches the worm.

When the cat is away the mice will play.

Every dog has its day.

No news is good news.

Once bitten twice shy.

A miss is as good as a mile.

A rolling stone gathers no moss.

Where there's a will there's a way.

As well be hanged for a sheep as a lamb.

A small leak will sink a great ship.

We never miss the water till the well runs dry.

The least said the soonest mended.

People in glass houses should not throw stones.

Americanisms

The success of the film industry in Hollywood and the distribution of American films throughout Europe resulted in many new words and phrases entering the English language:

Crook

Phoney

Bootlegger

Racket

Rubberneck

Guy

Yes Man

Go getter

Set-up

Public Enemy No. 1

Hobo

Gangster

Sucker

World War I and II also helped to introduce new words to our language. During World War I, the term 'blimp' was first used to describe a small airship. Other words which were introduced include:

Camouflage   *U-boat*

Big noise   *Civvy*

Zero hour

New words which gained common usage during World War II include:

Black market   *Backroom boys*

Blockbuster   *Airstrip*

Jeep   *Blitz*

Quisling   *Fifth column*

Blackout   *Dambuster*

Check the meaning and derivation of 'Quisling' and 'Fifth Column' in your dictionary. You may also need to refer to an appropriate history book or ask your history teacher.

Make a list of any words which you think have come from more recent films and television.

It is not unusual to have the same object referred to differently in Ireland/England and in America.

For example, in England and Ireland we say 'biscuits' whereas Americans would say 'cookies'.

Other examples:

ENGLISH WORD	AMERICAN WORD
nappies	*diapers*
film	*movie*
braces	*suspenders*
dust bin	*trash can*
fridge	*ice box*

Can you think of the word we use for the following items?

sidewalk	*gasoline*	*schedule*
elevator	*candy*	*drugstore*
fender	*faucet*	*trunk (of car)*

From the Australian 'soaps' and films you have seen compile ten Australian expressions used by Irish teenagers today.

Euphemisms

'That by which an unpleasant or offensive thing is given a milder term.'

The word 'euphemism' comes from the Greek *eu* meaning good/well and *pheme* meaning speaking. So this means that you want something unpleasant to sound well so you choose mild and gentle ways of describing situations.

For example, some might consider it too harsh or too blunt to say a person has died or is dead, so instead they use one of the following euphemisms for death:

- gone to her/his reward

- passed away

- no longer with us.

These are all euphemisms for death so the person is speaking euphemistically.

In our society we tend to be afraid to speak directly about serious illness or death. We are often embarrassed by references to sex. In these situations, euphemisms thrive.

Match each euphemism from the column on the left with its correct meaning in the column on the right:

EUPHEMISM	MEANING
Under the influence	To spit
Financially embarrassed	Undertaker
Perspiration	Contraception
Family planning	Drunk
Homemaker	Toilet
Funeral director	Pregnant
With child	Housewife/husband
Bathroom	Stupid
Expectorate	Broke
Intellectually challenged	Sweat

Neologisms

As we have already said, English is constantly being enriched and changed. The advances in Science, Technology and Space Exploration have introduced many new words to our vocabulary.

Neologisms are New Words.

Neologisms should not be confused with **slang** or **jargon**. Neologisms are new words which have achieved widespread accepted use. They are not catch-phrases or buzz words which enjoy a brief popularity.

An interesting example of a neologism is the word **scuba** as in scuba diving. Originally, the letters S.C.U.B.A. were abbreviations for: Self-Contained Underwater Breathing Apparatus. Eventually S.C.U.B.A., through widespread usage, became accepted as scuba.

Find the meaning of the following Neologisms. Put each in a sentence to show clearly that you understand what it means:

Union bashing	Tail back
Videodisc	Carer
Software	Teflon
Encapsulate	Radar

Tautology

Tautology is defined as: 'The unnecessary repeating of the same idea in different words' or the use of words that (especially needlessly) say the same thing. To say 'the old antique table was very valuable' is **tautology** because the word 'antique' implies that it is old. The word 'old' is redundant in the sentence as it has no function.

To say 'I, myself, believe . . . .' is plainly repeating the same meaning in different words.

Rewrite the sentences below omitting all redundant expressions:

- The Unions decided to merge together.

- The Army retreated back to the camp.

- Every single individual person should learn how to give artificial respiration.

- All the young babies were weeping tearfully.

- Every exile wishes to return back to the land of her/his birth.

The chief way of increasing your word power is to read. Join your local library. Reading is an adventure, it is also a source of enjoyment and of ideas. The better your vocabulary the easier it will be to express your ideas.

Remember—learning is a lifelong process.